Devotions for Couples in
Blended Families

Devotions for Couples in Blended Families

Margaret Smith-Broersma

kregel
RESOURCES

Grand Rapids, MI 49501

Devotions for Couples in Blended Families

Copyright © 1996 by Margaret Smith-Broersma

Published by Kregel Resources, an imprint of Kregel
Publications, P.O. Box 2607, Grand Rapids, MI 49501.
Kregel Resources provides timely and relevant resources for
Christian life and service. Your comments and suggestions
are valued.

Unless otherwise indicated, Scripture taken from the *Holy
Bible*: *New International Version*®. Copyright © 1973, 1978,
1984 by International Bible Society. Used by permission of
Zondervan Publishing House. All rights reserved.

Cover photograph: © THE STOCK MARKET/
                            Michael Keller 1995
Cover design: Alan G. Hartman
Book design: Nicholas G. Richardson

Library of Congress Cataloging-in-Publication Data
Smith-Broersma, Margaret.
   Devotions for couples in blended families: living and lov-
ing in a new family / Margaret Smith-Broersma.
      p.   cm.
   1. Married people—Prayer—books and devotions—
English. 2. Stepfamilies. I. Title.
BV4596.M3S65   1996   242'.644—dc20   96-10726
                                                                    CIP

ISBN 0-8254-3730-x

Printed in the United States of America
1 2 3 4 5 / 00 99 98 97 96

To my faithful husband, Roger, without whose
strength and love neither our blended family nor this book
would exist.

To all of my children—I am thankful I get to be the mom of all of
you: Aaron, Andrew, Tamara, Rebecca, and Lisa.

With gratitude to Nancy Hollowell and Dick Housekamp,
counselors who made a huge difference. If not for your wise counsel
and intervention, I shudder to think how
"unblended" we would be.

And most of all, thanks and glory to the Lord God,
Ruler of our lives, without Whom we would have no hope or praise or
a blended family.

◆

I would like to express my thanks to the many stepparents who
shared their stories with me. Every blended family is unique and each
one is precious in the sight of God. The names of individuals and the
details of their stories have been changed in some cases to protect their
privacy. Other individuals have graciously given me permission to identify them by their actual names.

Thanks is due also to my family who has given permission for many
of our stories to be shared.

Contents

"I can do all things through Christ, who strengtheneth me"
(Philippians 4:13 KJV).

Prologue:
Letters for the Worst Days

◆

The following letters were written for some special friends of mine.
Theirs is not a family exactly like mine, but then again, they are not so
different either. Perhaps the words that I wrote for them will be an
encouragement to some of you too.

To Her:

Dear Stepmom,

I think I know. It goes something like this:

His children plus your children equals more children than you think
you can possibly love. You are saying bad things in your head (and
maybe even out loud when pressed and desperate enough). "How did
I get so many kids? How did it happen that all of these needy creatures are filling up my house, making messes, disrupting the peace, not
doing anything I think they should—just generally acting like the individuals that they all are, all under my feet and feeding on my patience and my nerves and my food and my understanding of the human
race and sapping my strength and otherwise using me up? Like so many
leeches. How? Why did I do this? It's been (fill-in-the-blank) number
of years. But on this day, there is no love. I want to scream and run or
hide. I want the simple life of just my kids and me. But here we all
are.

"Was the woman, full of nurturance and love, thinking, 'Sure we
can, I love him,' was that woman me? And where has she gone? How
did she turn into the banshee that is me today?

"The Creator said that He took a look and saw this man and said,
'It is not good that he should be alone.' And so He sent me across his
path. His smell wows my senses and draws me nearer. His touch feels
like home again after a long time of wandering. Before we ever touch,
I know he will fill the empty spaces of my life and me his—like a
puzzle. We are two pieces who were wandering separately, and as soon
as we meet know that we will fit together and complete the whole—
fill the hole in my heart and in my life. WARNING! screams my head.
He doesn't come alone. He has children.

"But I sample their life as best I can, and they are so sweet and so
needy. Surely they just need to be organized by a great organizer like
me. Surely if we blend our lives, they will fit into the periphery of our

love and make a blue sky and nice accent colors—around the edges—probably. Besides, he can be responsible mostly for his and I for mine.

"But when we join, they are not staying in place. They scream, as children will, for center position, to be the focal point. There is that from-the-beginning-of-time quest by each of them to dominate, steal all the time and attention—from him—from me—until it feels like they are bloodsuckers and robbers of all our love. They are total users of the person that was me.

"My eyes look at their faces, and my mind evaluates their need. They are just children. They long only for love and approval (unconditional) like all beings on the earth. But somehow they do not seem like innocents to me. They are gaping, endless holes of need that reach out and continually suck at me for attention and love. I wail, 'I'm just no saint! I have nothing left to give!' And the man is hurting because I'm not loving his offspring like a mother 'should.' But that's the catch. They aren't mine, are they?

"I've been waiting for the mother-love to flood me like it did when my own tiny ones were placed in my arms. I thought I had it, but where did it go? Sucked up, used up. The tiredness, and the endless hungry mouths—and they don't like what I cook—and the endless dirty clothes and the endless mess and the endless violation of my space and their sapping of my strength and the wearing down of my patience and the stubborn independent 'I am a person too, look at me whoop-pee' noises reduce me to—nothing.

"That's what I think I've become. That once creative, intelligent woman has been reduced to a pool of used up organic matter sitting here inert on the floor—a puddle—nothing more—in the house that used to feel like mine.

"'God, if You're still there,' a small voice (very diminished almost evaporated) cries, 'help me.'"

But He's not home right now. And neither are you.

Tune in tomorrow. Will help come?

I'll write more later,
Margaret

To Him:

Dear Stepdad,

You are hurting. You were just trying to please her and look where it got you. You're hurting because your children are hurting. The woman that you married just doesn't seem to love them. Sure they're stinking and messy and screamy and needy. You shrug, "They're kids, what did you expect?"

You saw and felt their vulnerability; you wanted to protect them, but you saw her. You knew she would fit into the hole in your life, and so you put those little creatures that you love as much as you love the flesh of your own body into her house. You tried to mix that mystery of your longing for her (drat! why did I need her so bad?) into the pain of your half-life, and the wonderfulness only lasted until "I do."

You are bewildered and hurt. You brought this woman into your life, and you really meant it when you said, "Leaving all others, I will cleave only unto you." But the children keep getting in the way of the cleaving. And how can she fill the empty hole in your life when she can't quite fit over the spaces those kids keep opening up between you?

I'm sorry for your pain.

Here's my advice (called "been there"): Cry to God. Ask Him for a miracle. A miracle of love. Love enough for all those kids and for her too. All of it unconditional, all of it supernatural. No person has enough flesh or love for this; it must be from Him. Totally give your life, her needs, and the children's unending need to Him. Fill your mind with wisdom from His Word; refill every day. Say over and over, "Not my will, Lord, but Yours be done in my life and in my home."

He will answer. Check out James, chapter 1, about troubles, and Psalm 118:1–7 about His unfailing, endless love, and Psalm 25 for guidance. He will inject you with it. Check out Proverbs; it is full of wisdom. Any man who searches after wisdom will find it, and you will.

Here's a blessing: "Go in peace. And may the God of all wisdom and understanding fill you with supernatural wisdom, endless patience, and abounding strength and love to bear more of the children's needs so your wife (life) can be restored."

God bless you, I care.

Love,
Margaret

To Her:

Dear Stepmom:

I'm back. Guess what? Even though it sounded like God wasn't listening yesterday, He really was and He really did hear you. Here's my advice (called "been there"): Shut off the feelings a minute. They are, after all, what has overwhelmed and defeated you. Think a minute, preferably in the morning before you're all used up.

God says He's there. "My flesh and my heart may fail, but God is the strength of my heart and my portion forever" (Psalm 73:26). "Why are you downcast, oh my soul? Why so disturbed within me? Put your hope in God, for I will yet praise him, my Savior and my God" (Psalm 43:5). "I will never leave you or forsake you. So we say with confidence, 'The Lord is my helper; I will not be afraid'" (Hebrews 13:5–6). Think on those TRUTHS all the time.

God says, "My way is perfect and my plan the best for you." No, it doesn't feel like it right now. But He also says, "My strength is sufficient for you for my strength is made perfect in your weakness" (2 Corinthians 12:9). Only when you ARE totally used up and at the end of yourself will you feel HIS strength and love begin to flow through you. His resources are new every morning.

You—all used up and in a puddle on the floor—can be restored to life as you pour heaps of truth from His Word and the sustenance of His love into your life.

The kids grow up. (I promise!) Their needs get smaller. You may not be their mom, but you are a woman who can love them and add to their life. Just remember to keep yourself filled up from the One who is the Source.

I will pray for you to be filled with miraculous-beyond-yourself love and patience and gentleness that is not from you at all because you really don't have what it takes. But God does—Christ in you the hope of glory.

I care. I will pray every day.

Love,
Margaret

1
Will We Blend?

◆

May the Lord make your love increase and
overflow for each other (1 Thessalonians 3:12a).

I have clear memories of the father of my sons and me, together, watching our children. There we are, adoring them as they sleep or play, and thinking, "Surely, they are the brightest, the best, the most beautiful—the ultimate symbol of our union, the offspring of our united flesh." Their father was always so proud of them—a real "that's my boy" sort of dad.

> *Blending occurs only after great effort to be a part of one another's lives.*

Now I am married to someone else. The children we share did not spring from our union. This husband did not hold my children in their newborn wonder—nor did I hold his. Those infant years of bonding are missing from our history together as a family. How then do *we* stand together and gaze at these children we are blending into a new family?

Time passes. Though we do not share in their flesh, we share in their lives; and the day comes when one of us relates a tale, and we laugh and roll our eyes, enjoying "our" child. We watch the kids in action and look at each other with that knowing parental eye, acknowledging "wasn't that typical of them?"

We have become bonded in spirit, mind, and soul with these children as surely as if we had shared in their conception and birth. It has not been "natural." It does not happen "automatically." Blending occurs only after great effort to be a part of one another's lives, to present a united parental front, to consciously say, "I will be your wife/husband and the mother/father of your children," and then be it—even when it feels more like a burden than a joy. And one day we are surprised by the gladness, by the sharing, by the lightning revelation that we are together the parents of these wonderful children, no matter what their seed.

◆

Dear heavenly Father, thank You for giving us more children than we thought
we wanted or believed we were capable of raising. Thank You for surprising us
with the joy of love for them all. In Jesus' name, amen.

2

For a Not-So-Blended Day

◆

"Every . . . household divided against itself will not stand" (Matthew 12:25).

"Now I appeal to you, brothers and sisters, by the name of our Lord Jesus Christ, that all of you be in agreement and that there be no divisions among you, but that you be united in the same mind and the same purpose" (1 Corinthians 1:10 NRSV).

Sometimes it is shocking how fast we can revert to being a "divided camp." One parent sides with a birthchild against the other parent, or a child puts a guilt trip on a stepparent for not getting his or her way, and stepparents feel the unspoken accusation: "You favor your own."

> *It's shocking how fast we can revert to being a "divided camp."*

How can a stepparent really "understand"? The fact is, as we have grown to trust one another's motives, we do live less and less in a divided house. But short accounts must be kept when we feel hurt or offended. We need to clear things up as quickly as possible.

To tell the truth, I don't think we could have ever gotten over the discomfort of seeing another parent deal with "our" child if we had not sought out professional help. There were times we just couldn't believe the stepparent wasn't "wicked" and bound to damage our precious child. But the counselor was able to get us to express our feelings to each other.

When we were able to trust one another's motives and believe in the good we had in our hearts for each other's children, then we could relax and trust the stepparent to not do "harm." And when we see or hear things that make us feel offended or afraid once again, we talk about what lies behind our feelings.

So many stepfamilies we know have failed to blend. They either settled for living in a house as two separate families, or they divorced. Either way, their families suffer even more pain than the original losses that brought them together.

We have stubbornly refused to live as a divided family. But it has been tough and painful. Besides all the talk and counsel, we have prayed and prayed and had friends and relatives add their prayers to ours. But now, after more than eight years, we seldom feel like a divided house.

Through the power of all these things—prayer, God's grace, professional help, refusing to give up—we have come to trust one another's motives and understand one another's outlooks. Like any other married couple, we ride up and down on the waves of family life, but we are buoyed by the commitment and trust we have in one another. Meanwhile, the children grow, and we are living—successfully—in a blended family.

◆

Dear Father God, Sovereign Ruler of our lives, we bow before You in humble thanksgiving. It is a wonder that You saw fit to not just bring us together but to "blend us" into one family. We give You the honor and glory and praise for making this family work. Thank You. Amen.

3

Accepting My New Spouse
As a Parent to My Children

◆

"For I know the plans I have for you," declares the Lord, "plans to prosper you and not to harm you, plans to give you hope and a future" (Jeremiah 29:11).

". . . we also rejoice in our sufferings, because we know that suffering produces perseverance; perseverance, character; and character, hope" (Romans 5:3–4).

"For we are God's workmanship, created in Christ Jesus to do good works, which God prepared in advance for us to do" (Ephesians 2:10).

In 1982, when I had to have open-heart surgery, my biggest fear was not of death itself but fear of leaving my family alone. If I should die, who would raise my little sons, then four and six years old? Who would get to be the mother of my wonderful babies, nurture them and watch them grow? Who would love them as much as I did, the mom who was told she would never have them?

Before the new valve had to be put into my heart, I had time to gain complete trust in God. It didn't happen miraculously all in a moment. But by filling my mind with Scripture like those above and many others, I learned to give my boys, one day at a time, totally over to the Lord. I came to believe that if I did die, it would truly be God's plan for those children, the ones on whom He had His eye when they were yet unborn, the ones on whom He would keep His eye, even if I were gone.

During that first year of our blended family, their stepfather would sometimes reprimand them [my sons] for something that had not been wrong before. . . . When these situations occurred, my children and I would give each other a "look," conspirators against his "not understanding us."

Two years later, when their father was killed and I cried out, "What are You doing, God? How can I raise two male children without a father?" my previous lesson came to mind. OK, I hadn't died. But as surely as my death was not part of God's plan, now their father's death would leave its mark and become part of what would make them the men God had in mind for them to be.

Then Aaron and Andrew got a stepfather. Rog is quite different from their birthfather. During that first year of our blended family, before Rog and I had time to work out the differences between us, he would sometimes reprimand my sons for something that had not been wrong before. Or perhaps he would allow something that had previously been discouraged.

When these situations occurred, my children and I would give each other a "look," conspirators against his "not understanding us." As long as I continued to do this, the boys continued to resent and disrespect their stepfather and his authority in our home. But when I began to trust God and acknowledge to myself that this new man was just as much a part of God's plan for the character development of my children as I was, then I could encourage them to respect his wishes and obey him. When I trusted my children to God and also trusted them to their step-father, harmony in our home increased one hundred percent. At the same time my husband was learning to trust me to be the mother of his daughters.

I do not mean that an abusive situation should be tolerated as if it will be good character development for the children. But there is a wide range of what is acceptable and possible in adult-child relationships. Just because your new spouse's ways of doing things are different doesn't mean they are wrong.

We talked a lot about expectations—what I expected of Rog as a father, what he expected of me as a mother, whether we could live with those expectations, or where we may have to compromise. We each tried to act as a go-between, often explaining our child to the stepparent and the parent to the child. In addition to our own talking, the school social worker acted as a liaison between one son and his new dad on several occasions. When each learned what their actions and reactions brought out in the other, they learned to change their behavior. As our understanding of each other grew, so did our trust.

Just a few weeks ago one of my sons said to me, "I was remembering when you were first married. I remember that I really hated Dad. I wonder why? He is a really good dad for my brother and me. He is my discipliner and protector. He talks with us about life and stuff and helps us figure out what we should do and what we should be like. I wonder why I hated him back then, and I wonder why I changed?"

I felt my heart burst with joy! I reminded my child that when he got a new dad, he was only ten years old. He probably thought that everything would go back to being the way it was with his birthfather. But Rog was different. He didn't act in the other dad's old predictable ways. His idea of fun was not the same, nor were all his ideas of what was acceptable and unacceptable behavior the same. I suggested that in his disappointment at not finding his new dad to be the same as his birthfather, he hated him. But once they adjusted to each other, the hate was replaced with respect and, finally, with love.

◆

Dear Father in heaven, Sovereign of our lives, we pray that You will enable us to relax and trust our children to You. When we watch our new spouse with our children, make us wise enough to be able to tell the difference between "different" and "wrong." We thank You that You are at work in our lives and that you have a plan for our children that is being worked out.
In Jesus' name, amen.

4

It Takes Two Parents

◆

Two are better than one, because they have a good return for their work: If one falls down, his friend can help him up. But pity the man who falls and has no one to help him up! Also, if two lie down together, they will keep warm. But how can one keep warm alone? (Ecclesiastes 4:9–11).

Make every effort to keep the unity of the Spirit through the bond of peace (Ephesians 4:3).

I cannot emphasize enough the importance of always presenting a united front. It is impossible to agree on everything. But if one parent disagrees with the other's way of dealing with a child, discuss it privately, discuss it immediately, and if you cannot agree, discuss compromise. Never ever argue the treatment of a child within that child's hearing. A child's security comes from the stability of the marriage, and that security is undermined when a child finds him or herself the cause of dissension. One marriage has already ended, and the children need to know that no matter what the conflicts, this home will last.

One marriage has already ended, and the children need to know that no matter what the conflicts, this home will last.

The fact that their security depends upon it, however, does not stop children from intentionally trying to divide the parents.

The fact that their security depends upon it, however, does not stop children from intentionally trying to divide the parents. (This happens even in homes with all original members!) There is something about a kid, no matter how "sweet and innocent," that is really quite conniving and manipulative.

In the first weeks of our marriage my sons knew, when they gave me that "poor me" or "isn't this dumb" look, that they were getting me "on their side" against their stepdad. My attitude of "poor baby" just fed into their manipulations. But then I realized this behavior was actually keeping our family from blending and was damaging our new togetherness. We would never become one family at this rate!

But it was hard for them. After all, my boys and I were the ones who belonged together, had been together all their lives! How could it change to include these other people, and how does this man become a dad to them when he isn't anything like the dad they were used to? There really was enough love and loyalty for everyone, but they didn't know it then! They had to find out.

Boys are by no means the only children who try to come between parents. In order to be the center of attention, in order to feel sure that she has her daddy's love and devotion, a daughter will compete with a mother.

But when the mother is a stepmother, the competition is increased many times. Not only is the daughter testing her dad's loyalty to her, she is also wondering if deep inside he still loves her birthmother. I will never forget the moment when a social worker turned to me and asked, "Have you ever heard of the Oedipus complex?"

"Of course!" I felt a little foolish for not having thought of this myself.

And then she gently reminded me, "You've already won. He's your husband."

Please, dads, for the security of your home, back your wife while still showering tons of love and affection on your daughter. Just as I had to trust my children to their stepfather's authority, you may have to remind your child that your wife is the mom of THIS house and what she says goes here.

We recognized the need to present a united front, but at first we were afraid of what "damage" the stepparent might do to our child. To handle this insecurity we agreed on a code. When we said to our spouse, "May I see you in the bedroom?" we agreed we would come immediately. In the bedroom we would privately express our fears.

Surprisingly, and much to our relief, I think we only used the code once or twice. It just shows that the threat was more perceived than actual. What we really needed was time to grow in trust, trust in that other parent. Though his or her technique may be different, it really wasn't going to damage our kid.

Someday all of the children will grow up and leave home. Our marriage is what will be left. Will it be whole or hopelessly divided from the divisions over the children?

————◆————

Dear God, thank You that You invented marriage not only for husband and wife but also to give our children a safe and secure home in which to grow. Please help us to maintain a united parental front for the strength of our marriage and the unity of our family. In Jesus' name we pray, amen.

5
Custom Stepdad

◆

Though I am free and belong to no man, I make myself a slave to everyone, to win as many as possible. . . . I have become all things to all men so that by all possible means I might save some. I do all this for the sake of the gospel, that I may share in its blessings (1 Corinthians 9:19–23).

Therefore I do not run like a man running aimlessly (1 Corinthians 9:26a).

I n our wedding vows we said, "and I will be the mother/ father of your children." Wow! What a pledge that turned out to be! But the truth is, many stepparents who read this book are not going to be the primary parent of their spouse's children. The children may

You may relate to your stepchildren as friend, confidant, actual parent figure, or mentor and a role model.

have a birthmother or father, and the stepparent is someone who is parenting in *addition* to the birthparent, not replacing the birthparent. There are many different roles a stepparent may choose and, as with a birthparent, the roles may change as the children grow.

We have friends whose blended family consists of a mom with older teenagers and a dad with a preschooler and early elementary kids. While it is fairly easy for her to see that she basically has to "do the mommy thing" with his kids when they are home, what can he be to her kids who are almost grown up? How can he be a "custom stepdad"?

Stepparents and counselors Elizabeth Einstein and Linda Albert say that you may relate to your stepchildren as friend, confidant, actual parent figure, or mentor and a role model. They also say that in their counseling experience, "the stepparents who define their role as that of friend are usually the most satisfied and successful."* The fact is, in many stepparenting situations, the children already have a mom and a dad.

Bob was a guy who was very set on being a good father for his new wife's children. Bob and Sally had decided not to have children together so they could do a good job with Sally's older children. The problem was the kids wanted Bob to be their friend. They had a father with whom they spent time, and they rejected Bob's attempts at discipline and other "fatherly" overtures.

They did, however, enjoy fishing and hunting with their stepdad, and as a family, they were wild about the great vacations they took together.

Bob was a voracious reader and always had plenty of input about the places they visited. At these times they thoroughly enjoyed being together. But back at home Bob would get angry and frustrated because the kids didn't respect him like a "real" father and didn't accept his discipline.

The kids and their mom had lived alone for so long, they had their own hierarchy of power with discipline structures already in place. Because of this established order, they didn't need Bob in the way *he wanted* to be needed. Fortunately, a sharp counselor was able to point out to Bob what he really had going for him.

The kids actually liked him. They accepted him completely as a mentor and confidant, talking over their life decisions with him and looking to him for guidance on things from cars to dates. In fact, as long as he didn't attempt to be the disciplinarian but left that up to Sally, with whom they had spent most of their formative years, they actually had a good relationship.

When Bob relaxed and enjoyed the relationship they had, both he and the children were less frustrated, and there was more peace in their home. When he stopped forcing a relationship, he actually did become, by backing up their mother, more involved in the discipline—but got less resentment!

As a confidant and mentor, say the counselors, a stepparent can provide a needed adult sounding board. If you can win their trust, the teen who may be struggling for independence from a birthparent, but still needs adult guidance, may well turn to you, the stepparent, for support. You may very well be able to transmit values and beliefs to your stepchildren in a role as confidant and mentor. To be a mentor and confidant a stepparent has to purposefully take on that role and develop that type of relationship with the stepchild, who in turn must desire it.*

The stepparent as role model is another story—you *are* a role model whether you want to be or not! Any adult involved in a child's life on a regular basis becomes a role model from whom that child may pick up attitudes and model behavior. Even if your stepchild claims to hate you and doesn't seem to want a relationship with you, he or she is watching and learning from you all the time. Does this feel like a burden? Einstein and Albert challenge stepparents to look upon this as an *opportunity*. You are the one who chooses to make your influence as role model positive or negative.

As the years pass, your role in your stepchild's life will change, just as it does for a birthparent. The challenge is finding the role that is right for both of you for *now*. Be sensitive to what that child needs; be flexible. If you need to learn about a new sport or game to be that child's friend—do it!

I don't mean you must act like a kid or teenage pal to your stepchild.

But what I do mean is that it is up you, the adult, to take an interest in the kid, to initiate the time spent together. The stepchild may refuse your overtures of friendship, especially at first. But be available, be there, and try to show that that child is important to you by willingly and purposefully sharing in his or her life.

Be there for your stepchildren and watch each relationship develop in its own unique way. The apostle Paul "became all things to all men" so that he could relate the Gospel to them in a way they would understand.

To be a successful stepparent you may have to be different things at different times to different children. But you certainly can't be a good parent or stepparent by running aimlessly along; you must purpose in your heart to work on a relationship, whatever style it may be.

———————◆———————

Dear Lord, teach me to be what my stepchildren need. Give me wisdom to know how to relate to each one of them. Thank You for the promises of wisdom and of strength we find in Your Word. In Jesus' name, amen.

*Elizabeth Einstein and Linda Albert, *Strengthening Your Stepfamily* (Circle Pines, Minn.: American Guidance Service, 1986), 34–37.

6

Blended Discipline

◆

For all who are led by the Spirit of God are children of God. For you did not receive a spirit of slavery to fall back into fear, but you have received a spirit of adoption. When we cry, "Abba! Father!" it is that very Spirit bearing witness with our spirit that we are children of God (Romans 8:14–15 NRSV).

No discipline seems pleasant at the time, but painful. Later on, however, it produces a harvest of righteousness and peace for those who have been trained by it (Hebrews 12:11).

I n devotion 3, I talked about how I had to trust my sons to God, and that meant learning to accept their stepfather as their disciplinarian. Some families, especially those with older children, may opt for the solution that I talked about in devotion 5 in which the stepparent is a friend but not really

If you don't decide what kind of parent to be to your stepchild and you just let things slide, you will indeed be no parent at all.

a parent to the stepchildren, which means he or she is not their main disciplinarian. But the truth is, if you want the family that lives under one roof to be a blended family, one family living together as a unit with a mom and a dad at the head of that family, the birthparent and the children will have to allow the stepparent to be active in the discipline of the children in some way.

It may be important, in the beginning of the family, for the natural parent to do most or all of the disciplining. Again, it depends very much on the age of the children. The younger they are, the more it is necessary, and perhaps even more natural, for both the parent and the stepparent to do the disciplining. If a stay-at-home mom is stepparent to younger children, obviously she must also be the disciplinarian simply because she is there.

In his book, *Living in a Stepfamily Without Getting Stepped On*, Kevin Leman says that you should "start out with each parent disciplining their own children."* As was true for us, he finds that the birthmother has the most difficult time in allowing the stepfather to discipline her kids. "If," he says, "she has been living for some time as a single mom, it's not unusual for her to have slipped into a permissive approach."† In other cases, of course, it may be the birthfather that is lax in setting limits with his children.

Whatever the case, even if you do start out with the birthparent disciplining his or her own children, this should be a short-term situation. Dr. Leman says that "in the long run you want to find a system where both of you can discipline all the children consistently and lovingly."‡ Family members can work into their roles a little at a time. Love and discipline must be balanced with allowing time to work into a natural relationship. Time for love to grow is needed before the discipline starts.

All of us who believe in Jesus as our Savior are adopted children of God. The Scriptures tell us that if we are true children, then He will discipline us in the same way that a real loving parent will discipline his or her child. If we are serious about being real parents to our stepchildren, then we must learn, first of all, to love our stepchildren and, second of all, to discipline them fairly.

As Dr. Leman says, work into it gradually as you win the trust of the children. You may choose not to be their parent but their friend. Whatever you decide, do it willfully and with intention. Because if you don't decide what kind of parent to be to your stepchild and you just let things slide, you will indeed be no parent at all.

You may want to begin by asking, "What do these children need?" If both their birthparents are active in their lives and are effective disciplinarians, if the children are secure and under control, you may opt to be their friend. But kids need two parents. If you are all they have, then purpose in your heart, asking wisdom from God, to love them and discipline them as your own. If you do, the day may come when they will call you "Daddy, Father" or "Mommy, Mother," words describing a relationship of intimacy and trust, just like Romans 8:15 says.

◆

Dear Father in heaven, the Perfect Parent and most awesome Example of love and discipline, we come to You, asking You to fill us with love and wisdom for this task of disciplining our stepchildren. May we be effective parents in their lives, for their good and for Your glory we pray, amen.

---

*Dr. Kevin Leman, *Living in a Stepfamily Without Getting Stepped On* (Nashville: Nelson, 1994), 23.

†Leman, *Living in a Stepfamily,* 208.

‡Ibid.

7

One Kid's View of a Stepparent

◆

Show me your ways, O Lord, teach me your paths; guide me in your truth and teach me, for you are God my Savior, and my hope is in you all day long (Psalm 25:4—5).

If any of you lacks wisdom, he should ask God, who gives generously to all without finding fault, and it will be given to him. But when he asks, he must believe and not doubt (James 1:5—6a).

In considering what kind of stepparent each of us needs to be, I talked to Josh, a young man who spent his final growing up years in a blended family. We discussed a lot of things, many of them positive and some not so positive. The best thing, Josh said, about living in a blended family was that he was never bored or lonely! There was always something going on and someone to hang out with. But the hardest thing, he said, was getting a stepdad.

When she remarried, she hoped that her new husband, who seemed very strong, would be able to lend the firm hand that her adolescent son needed. But there was no way her son was going to ac cept this hand in his life!

First of all, as a young teenage boy, Josh was oblivious to the needs his mother had for a husband. He thought his sisters, mom, and he got along just fine the way they were. He was the "man of the house," why did she even need to remarry? Josh's father died when he was fourteen, and many people told him things like, "Now you have to take care of your mom" or "Now you are in charge." He had taken them seriously.

Of course his new father didn't see Josh that way. His stepfather saw him as a cocky sixteen-year-old who wanted to be in control but demonstrated his selfishness and immaturity in many ways. Josh saw himself as his mother's protector and the man of the family, but he also admits he was rebellious and could give his mom a real hard time.

When she remarried, Beth hoped that her new husband, Steve, who seemed very strong, would be able to lend the firm hand that her adolescent son needed. But there was no way Josh was going to accept this hand in his life! His anger and resistance toward Steve were clear from the beginning.

Because is was so obvious how Josh felt, for the most part Steve backed off and left the discipline to Beth. But times would arise when, for the peace of the household and the well-being of his wife, Steve felt he had to step in. For a couple of years the hostility increased as this young man competed with his stepfather for dominance and control in their home. One day, in the midst of a terrible argument, they actually came to blows. Not being a violent family, they have only told this story to a few people.

It all began in the usual manner of parent-child conflict—Josh thought he was being treated unfairly by his stepfather. But in the passion of that awful hour of conflict, as they hit and punched each other, those two men were able to finally communicate. Beth says that they finally learned where the other stood. After this confrontation, things were permanently changed, fortunately for the better. Steve ended up apologizing for his harshness and for losing control. Josh also felt ashamed of his hostility and said so. But from the young man's point of view, that day his stepdad allowed him to grow up.

Josh says he was treated differently from then on. Soon after the big fight, he was given responsibilities that no other sibling had—like keys to the family business and being entrusted with the weekly washing of the trucks that belonged to that business. He said, "Here I was, a smart-aleck kid just out of high school, and my stepdad trusted me enough to let me drive those rigs around the lot and wash and repark them. And he didn't even check up on me! It was awesome to be trusted like that!"

The respect, he says, became mutual. He had seen himself as the protector of his mother and sisters, a role usurped by the intruding stepfather. Being displaced meant that he was defensive of his mother where no offense was intended. He would often feel angry for what he viewed as unfair treatment of his mother by his stepfather. After being allowed to "grow up," he realized that his mom and her husband actually had a good marriage, and he saw that he had been jealous. Once he was given his own place of importance in the family, he no longer needed to be in competition with his stepfather.

Josh says that he will always grieve the loss of his birthdad. The relationship he has with his stepfather is one of friendship and respect, not at all like the one of emotional warmth and intimacy he remembers having with his birthparent. But it is good, he says, to be friends with his stepdad. He decided to call him "pop" because the name worked for them. They are two men who love and respect one another. A stepfamily is not a nuclear family. It will always be different, but that doesn't mean it can't be wonderful in its own unique way.

The challenge to each stepparent is finding your own brand of "wonderful," your own way to relate to each stepchild. This may differ greatly for each of them depending on their age, sex, and place in the family.

On top of it all, I cannot imagine doing the tough job of stepparenting without the wisdom of God's Word, the support of prayer, and the presence of the Holy Spirit in the blended home.

◆

Dear Lord Jesus, live and rule in our blended family. Teach us how to parent each child that lives here. May we do it well, wisely, and with love. Thank You for being in all of this with us. In Jesus' name, amen.

8
This Too Shall Pass (Stages)

◆

There is a time for everything, and a season for every activity under heaven (Ecclesiastes 3:1).

But I trust in you, O LORD; I say, "You are my God." My times are in your hands (Psalm 31:14–15a).

I t is Saturday—car-wash day. Rog backs the car out of the garage and parks it in the driveway. Then he goes back into the garage, drags out the hose, fills the bucket, adds detergent, and begins one of his favorite rituals. First one car and then the other begins to shine, belying the fact that they both have over a hundred thousand miles on them. Sometimes a kid helps; sometimes a kid washes not only his or her own car but ours too. But this is something my husband enjoys doing, and he doesn't feel like he's caring for our autos well unless he "goes over them" at least every two weeks.

As cute as kids are, they're a whole lot cuter and the story's a whole lot funnier when it's happening to the guy across the street rather than to me!

On this lovely fall day while doing this task, he notices the guy across the street trying to wash his car too. Our neighbor's three little boys are "helping." Like Rog, he fills the pail with warm water and detergent. He washes down a side, his sons following with their own sponges or rags. As he goes around to the other side, one boy picks up the hose and starts spraying. Of course the water arches over the car, drenching his dad. Dad runs back around the car to stop the hose sprayer, instructs the kid in what to do, and attempts to resume the job.

Shortly Rog hears a crash, splash, and loud and angry crying. The youngest child has attempted to go wading in the pail, has dumped it over, and the middle brother, angered by the loss of soapy water, is alternately beating on and spraying his little brother. The oldest one jumps up and down, yelling and screaming about the events and trying to separate his siblings. With a shake of his head, the young father gives up on the car wash for now. Maybe he'll squeeze it in later when the children are less interested in "helping."

Rog comes into the house grinning and reports the events of car-wash day in our neighborhood. "You know," he says, "I think I really enjoy the fact that our kids are teenagers! I remember those days when our little kids tried to help, and as cute as kids are, they're a whole lot cuter and the story's a whole lot funnier when it's happening to the guy across the street instead of me!"

We then reminisced about the many stages our children have gone through. Every stage had its own frustrations, but each has had its own joys. We recalled absolutely loving their young years when they were excited about everything. It was so much fun to enter into their discovery of life. But the work! The diapers, the food messes, the habitually dirty faces, and the frustration and fatigue of simply remembering everything for everybody.

Now, the teen years are scary in a lot of ways. But teenage kids are so neat to talk to—young adults to old adults. They have become self-conscious about their enthusiasm for things and are embarrassed by their parents' exuberance at times, but they are also a lot less work and remember, at least theoretically, many more things for themselves. As much as we miss a certain childish stage, we realize we are really enjoying them now. Thus, every phase of our children's development tends to be a time of loss and rediscovery. Yes, we would say that raising children is a process of continual loss as we watch them pass through the various stages of growth and development. Just as we get used to the kids being a certain way, they take another step ahead on the road of life and keep changing, until eventually, as with two already, we have to let them go completely into adulthood.

As my Smith mother-in-law used to say when I complained about rashes, runny noses, or fighting, "Oh, Margaret, this too shall pass!" She's right. It passes. I hope we have entered fully into and enjoyed completely, all the stages of our children's lives before it is too late.

———◆———

Dear Jesus, thank You for all the stages our children go through as we watch them grow up. Help us to enjoy every one of them. Please bless our children, Lord. May they be faithful to You in all the times of their lives. In Your name, amen.

9
Once Blended—Always Blended

◆

. . . you will be called by a new name that the mouth of the Lord will bestow (Isaiah 62:2b).

But now, this is what the Lord says—"Fear not, for I have redeemed you; I have summoned you by name; you are mine" (Isaiah 43:1).

When we look at our wedding pictures, we see a group that sort of "matches." We look like we belong together. When we were first married, people would look at our picture and try to guess which kid was whose by birth and often got it wrong. Because of this, we naively thought the day would come when

> *We naively thought the day would come when people we knew would forget and new people we met would never know that we are stepparents.*

people we knew would forget and new people we met would never know that we are stepparents. But the truth is we are—and always will be—a blended family. That is the "name" for our kind of family.

Besides the obvious fact that our children have different last names, we often have to explain how we got so many children in such a short time. Introductions to new people usually go something like this:

"Hi, my name is Margaret/Roger. My job is teacher/manager; we have five kids."

"Oh? (!) How old are they?"

"18, 17, 16, 16, 14."

"Oh? (!!)" A confused look, a twist of the head.

"Do you have twins?"

"No. They're eight weeks apart. You see, we have a blended family. We were both widowed and . . ."

And so it goes—the surprise at the big family and their ages and the explanation. And we remain—always—a blended family. That's what we're called, that's what we are, and it's OK. Not only are we not second-rate, we are special. God has done many miracles to bring us together, to make us one, to make us the family that we are.

But most people don't grasp the idea of widowhood in people our age. (Obviously, as we get older, this question is less frequent than it used to be.)

As if denying what they just heard and not ready to accept the idea of widowhood in a thirty-something adult, the next question usually is, "Do you have the children all the time?"

Then we have to repeat, "Both widowed. My husband was killed by a hit-and-run driver; his wife died of cancer."

Eight years later, the explanation of how we came to be a family is almost always a part of any introduction. We're not just a family, we're a blended family—we were especially put together by God. I hope that we will always give the praise and glory to Him.

◆

Dear Sovereign God, Ruler of our lives, thank You for changing our mourning into new joy. We praise you. Amen.

10
Strength to Cope

◆

So do not fear, for I am with you; do not be dismayed, for I am your God. I will strengthen you and help you; I will uphold you with my righteous right hand (Isaiah 41:10).

When we got married, it was spring, and the children finished the school year in their own schools. That meant I had to get out of the house early each day to ferry the boys to their school while the girls hitched a ride with the neighbors to their closer one. After school I would dash to get first one set of children

After school I would dash to get first one set of children and then the other. Both sets were sure I made them wait because I liked the other set of kids better.

and then the other. Both sets were sure I made them wait because I liked the other set of kids better.

In beautiful weather I would plead with the girls, "Can't you walk home? It's less than a mile."

"No."

And naively, I thought them too burdened with bags, too young to feel safe. The next year we had one school and a bus to go with it. And rather than ride the bus, more often than not, they would bike or walk! Sometimes, even in rainy cold weather, sometimes for no reason, here they would come, one or more of them, ambling along, enjoying their walk.

I thought, "GREAT! Now that there is a bus, they don't need me, so they walk! They could have walked last spring too, and I wouldn't have had to go through all that frustration and tension." But maybe the truth is, now that they were a little more sure that I cared for all of them; when they were a little more secure, they were free to walk home.

———— ◆ ————

Dear Jesus, thank You for seeing us through those demanding, tough times in the beginning of our new family. Thank You for the strength and patience and love You provided to get us started on the road as a blended family. In Your name, amen.

11
Confidence in Times of Uncertainty

◆

I can do all things through Christ who strengthens me
(Philippians 4:13 NKJV).

And my God shall supply all your need according to His riches in glory by
Christ Jesus (Philippians 4:19 NKJV).

I recall so poignantly the September morning I stood watching the children line up at the foot of our driveway in response to someone's yell of "Bus, bus." I am thinking, "Oh my! Where have all

> *Thank You, Lord, that I get to be the mom of all these kids.*

the children come from? Me, a would-be perfectionist, with not much patience for childish messiness—how did I end up with those five magnificent children lining up to meet the big yellow bus?"

All of them are waiting for their ride into what the new school-year will bring—while I watch from the window and then run to the bedroom for the camera. From that window I catch another glimpse and am overwhelmed by the realization that they—all of them—are my children, my responsibility.

As I see them get on the bus in the outfits we selected together, wearing the pigtails and bows and curls and coifs I did for them, and carrying the lunch boxes with lunches I made and notebooks I took them to the store to buy, I say out loud, "These are my children! How did I end up with five? Can I really do this job of raising all of them?"

Knowing their biggest pain is behind them but that they still carry a part of the grief that goes with all of us everywhere, I'm wondering how they will do in school this year. I offer a prayer for their safety and God's blessing. And really, one of thanks too, that I get to be the mom of "all these kids."

◆

Thank You, Lord, that I get to be the mom of all these kids. And when I think
I can't do it, I thank You that You are there with the strength and wisdom and
love that I lack. In Jesus' name, and for Your glory, amen.

12
One of the Best Days

◆

Then your light will break forth like the dawn, and your healing will quickly appear; . . . the glory of the LORD will be your rear guard. Then you will call, and the LORD will answer; you will cry for help, and he will say: Here am I (Isaiah 58:8–9).

Fast forward eight years from the bus scene in devotion 11. The little girl with tightly permed curls, sweet lacy blouse, and neat white knee socks who climbed on the bus that day is now a college-bound teen with correctly bobbed hair, perpetual blue jeans, and a newly acquired heartbreak.

> *And when I sit there, stroking her hair, rocking her back and forth, I know that I am her mom and she needs me.*

Tonight I leave the table and follow her into her bedroom where she is in tears. Just as naturally as breathing, I draw her into my arms, this girl-woman, and comfort her. I am thinking yes, yes. I remember the pain and confusion. After all, it was only just last week (Wasn't it?) that I was the jilted teen with the breaking heart! And when I sit there, stroking her hair, rocking her back and forth, I know that I am her mom and she needs me. Was there ever any doubt that she and I believed this? It's hard to remember.

The time flew by. Some of it (to be honest) in rage, some of it in pain, some of it in floods of joy and deep harmony between us. When did we learn to read each other's thoughts? We did. But now, on this eve of her adulthood, I know that I am her mom, and I, like no one else, know her heart. Her dad comes in and we pray for her. And we know how good it is and how blessed we are to be a two-parent home— to be there for our children. Yes. Our children.

It's not amazing to us that the experts are finally deciding what we knew when we got married: Kids need two parents, one of each sex. We know we could not, can not, do alone for our children what we can do together.

◆

Thank You, Father, for the strength, love, healing, binding, and blending that You have brought to our relationships. You alone are good and all wise, and You have worked and are working in our lives. You have truly answered us when we cried for help, and we praise You. In the name of Your glorious Son, our only Savior, amen.

13

It Takes Two Parents—
One of the Best Days

◆

My son, do not forget my teaching, but keep my commands in your heart, for they will prolong your life many years and bring you prosperity. Let love and faithfulness never leave you; bind them around your neck, write them on the tablet of your heart. Then you will win favor and a good name in the sight of God and man. Trust in the LORD with all your heart and lean not on your own understanding; in all your ways acknowledge him, and he will make your paths straight (Proverbs 3:1–6).

I grab my son for a playful tug-of-war, attempting to "get him" for picking on me. As we struggle playfully, I feel his strength and the new breadth of his shoulders. In surprise, I stand back and take a good look. With that brief investigation a split-second flood of questions rise in my mind: "When did he become a young man? When did he get stronger than I am? How is it that he still respects my authority? Does he know he's stronger?"

When in the beginning of our family we often "explained" our children to each other, now we find ourselves explaining the other's children.

I hope that he doesn't know. But of course he does. He felt my weakness as surely as I just felt his strength! Would this be a bad moment for us if I were still a single mom? Does knowing that there is a bigger and stronger male in the house make him feel protected and secure?

As I give him a parting kiss on the cheek (he is required by his age to show some reluctance but does so with a grin), I am thankful once again for all we have—five emotionally healthy teenagers who have had the benefit of being raised in a two-parent home. "Thank You, Lord."

Rog is grateful in the same sort of way whenever I tell him some female thing. "Boy! What's gotten into her? She's so sensitive!" And I remind him about PMS. A sheepish grin tells me how glad he is I am there to buy the clothing and paraphernalia necessary for our blossoming daughters. Oh how times change! When in the beginning of our family we often "explained" our children to each other, now we find ourselves explaining the other's children.

"Now wait a minute," he tells me. "There's nothing wrong with his doing that. It may seem silly to you, but trust me, it's a 'guy thing.' Why my brothers and I . . ."

Or I'll say, "Don't you see her body language, can't you read her countenance? She's really upset! Go ahead, talk to her. She wants you to."

I can say wholeheartedly: Despite the difficulties of "blending," we are more than grateful for our two-parent home.

◆

Dear God, thank You for bringing us together and staying with us always through all the necessary adjustments. You are good and faithful. For Your blessings we praise You. Amen.

14

The Second Marriage

♦

They celebrate your abundant goodness and joyfully sing of your righteousness
(Psalm 145:7).

"Remember the former things, those of long ago; I am God, and there is no
other; I am God, and there is none like me. . . . I say: My purpose will stand,
and I will do all that I please" (Isaiah 46:9–10).

We live with shadows. They are the memory, perhaps even the spirit, of our departed ones. Is there a day they don't flit around the edges of our lives, sometimes even coming to the center?

Can there be bright shadows?

These shadows do not dim the sweetness of our special moments but are included as part of what we are. Can there be bright shadows? A contradiction of terms surely, but an apt description.

Perhaps they would fade, but the children are living-flesh reminders. I see my first husband in the mouth, chin, and nose of one son. I see the temperament, interests, and attitudes—even his very words—in the other. How can this young man act and think so much like the dad he lost when he was only six?

While spring cleaning, I find pictures from the years of Rog's previous marriage. In those photos of his first wife I see my daughters, a chin and smile of one, the shoulders—and I suspect even the walk—of another. And old friends have informed me, "She's just like her mom!" No matter how much time passes, we continue to live with these reflections of our former loves.

When we feel something missing in our present love, each shortcoming is a reminder of the beautiful relationship we had and lost. Now we have different beautiful things. But despite how much we have now, how rich our lives, how at times we admit that our lives are even more to our satisfaction than before, the truth is, we simply do not have what we lost. And as that was very precious and loved, we will grieve the loss even as we rejoice in what we have.

The grief, though always with us, does not seem to diminish our joy. This marriage is quite simply a new and different thing, and the former one remains a part of who and what we are. We thank God for those bright shadows from the past who live with us, making us who we are and making our love what it is.

———————◆———————

Dear sovereign God, thank You for all that You have given in our old lives and in our lives now. Thank You that Your plan is best and that You are at work, even when we haven't known it or felt it. No words can express how great Your faithfulness has been toward us. Thank You for making us Your children. Our lives are in Your hands. We trust only in You for our tomorrows; we thank You and praise You for our yesterdays. In Your most blessed and holy name, we pray, amen.

15

On Being "the Other Mom"

◆

I can do all things through Christ who strengthens me (Philippians 4:13).

My brothers and sisters, whenever you face trials of any kind, consider it nothing but joy, because you know that the testing of your faith produces endurance;... If any of you is lacking in wisdom, ask God, who gives to all generously and ungrudgingly, and it will be given you
(James 1:2–3, 5 NRSV).

Even as I wrote devotion 14, I was well aware that most of the stepparents who read this book are not stepparents because of death but rather because of divorce. When I ask my divorced and remarried friends to share their biggest problems, one of the most common answers is "the ex."

Competition with the birthmother is almost unbearable. . . ."At my other house I don't have to _____, so why do I have to do it here?"

Marian, a stepmother friend, who married a man with custody of his young children, had to deal with their birthmother's screaming, "Why are you taking my babies from me?" when she had been the one to leave the family! Now the absent birthmother resents Marian's parenting.

Shelly, another stepmom friend, agrees that competition with the birthmother is almost unbearable. In this case the birthmother deserted the family as well, but as she lives nearby and sees the children often, Shelly lives with her biting comments and criticisms, which often hurt or confuse the children.

For example, "My mom says the ponytail you put in my hair yesterday was dumb. She likes it this way." Or, "My mom says I don't have to eat what I don't like, so I won't eat what you cook." And the most common, "At my other house I don't have to _____, so why do I have to do it here?"

Now how is a stepmother, no matter how patient, supposed to function with that kind of uphill battle over just about everything?

I do not have an answer. But I do have encouragement. God's Word is filled with wisdom, reassurance, and power. Fill your mind with applicable verses such as the ones above and others such as:

Psalm 66:10–12 Hebrews 10:30
Matthew 5:10–12 1 Peter 1:6–7
Romans 12:20–21 1 Peter 2:19–23
Ephesians 4:31–32 1 Peter 4:12–14

There are tons of encouragement in God's Word! Put these or your favorite encouraging verses from the Word on note cards, and read them over whenever you need them.

And "talk, talk, talk." Wives, tell your husbands how you feel. Husbands, open up and tell your wives what you're thinking. Custodial birthparent, go to your children and set some clear guidelines for how you expect them to treat their stepparent. You may want to tell them, "This is my husband/wife; in this house he/she is the dad/mom, so in this family, what he/she says is what goes." And yes, set some limits with the ex-spouse too. At least try to make him or her understand that critical, biting comments only hurt and confuse the children. See if you can get all the adults on the same team; the children will be the winners.

If you don't know where to set the limits or what reasonable expectations really are, do your talking with a Christian counselor. Many counselors do sessions with the whole family so that the children and parents can do some role playing. With help, your stepchildren can learn how their remarks make a parent feel. Parents can learn where to draw a line and stand firm, and where they need to give in.

You cannot control or change the "ex," but you can learn how to deal with the conflicts as a family. You can know how you stand with each other. You can become a family unit that has agreed upon how to relate to the noncustodial parent.

◆

Dear Father, thank You that You see every problem and understand every threat to our blended family even better than we see them ourselves. Thank You that although You don't promise that our lives will be easy, You do promise to never forsake us or leave us. In Jesus' name, amen.

16
Needed: Perseverance

◆

"Behold, I will rain bread from heaven . . . and the people shall go out and gather a certain quota every day, that I may test them . . ."
(Exodus 16:4 NKJV).

My brothers and sisters, whenever you face trials of any kind, consider it nothing but joy, because you know that the testing of your faith produces endurance; and let endurance have its full effect, so that you may be mature and complete, lacking nothing. If any of you is lacking in wisdom, ask God, who gives to all generously and ungrudgingly, and it will be given you
(James 1:2–5 NRSV).

I don't know about you, but I'm great in a crisis. It's the burdens of the persistent variety that get me down. In an emergency I rise to the moment, keep my composure, and do the right thing (usually). I learn all kinds of wonderful spiritual insights when hit with a test, but I have still to figure out what I was supposed to learn from some of the "long hauls" of my life. When my husband was killed, I "stood up"

> *I learn all kinds of wonderful spiritual insights when hit with a test, but have still to figure out what I was supposed to learn from some of the "long hauls" of my life.*

well. I cried and sobbed for an entire night. Once that was out of my system, I was able to face life; that is, I was able to think and act as the occasion required. Various people were pleased with my stamina and "bearing up." But in the long haul, in the day after day grind of life as a single parent, I did not do as well.

The long haul tested my faith, and in some ways it was found wanting. Friends of ours are just the opposite. When someone gets hurt or there is an emotional crisis of the childhood variety, say, a favorite toy is broken, all chaos reigns. The injured party begins to scream; everyone else starts to holler their solutions and their version of the crisis to the others. People run around like chickens with their heads cut off. If one is in a panic, they are all in a panic. If one screams, they all scream. It's quite a sight!

But over the long haul, this same family lives with pressures that I feel I simply could not endure. They find joy and peace every day while coping with long-term illnesses of not one, but *two* members of their family whom they visit in different care facilities *daily*. I feel I could not endure this type of demand on my time and emotions. But they have calmly accepted this and live around it like normal, happy people until the bizarre way they react when a crisis comes up again!

The children of Israel were given tests by God too. Some were of the crisis variety, and some were tests over "the long haul."

I began this section with Exodus 16:4. Believe it or not, the provision of their daily bread was a test! The Lord gave them manna in the wilderness, and every morning, day after day for forty years, that is what they gathered and that is what they ate.

As stepparents we face many tests of the long-haul variety. There may very well be an annoying ex-spouse that will not relent in his or her interference in your lives. There may be a stepchild that will not, no matter what, accept you. You or your child may have a physical problem that simply will never be gone and must be accepted as a part of your life. In his book, *The Second Wind*, Chuck Swindoll says, "The marathons—the relentless, incessant, persistent, continual tests that won't go away—ah, these are the ones that bruise but build character. The stronger the winds, the deeper the roots, and the longer the winds blow, the more beautiful the tree."*

This theme of character building is found again in the first chapter of James—my favorite passage on trials and suffering. These verses explain that it is the persistent testing of our faith that helps us develop character. It is the marathon of life that make us into the kind of people God wants us to be.

Remember, no matter what your circumstances—however long you may have to endure a testing of your faith—God is actively at work, making you into the strong and beautiful person He wants you to be.

◆

Dear God, You are "my rock and my fortress, in whom I trust." Strengthen me, enable me by Your grace and power to stand up to the persistent storms that blow over our blended family. Thank You. Amen.

---

*Chuck Swindoll, *The Second Wind* (Grand Rapids: Zondervan, 1977), 7.

17
Blending—a Process

◆

Therefore, if anyone is in Christ, he is a new creation: the old has gone, the new has come! All this is from God (2 Corinthians 5:17).

Perseverance must finish its work so that you may be mature and complete, not lacking anything (James 1:4).

Being confident of this, that he who began a good work in you will carry it on to completion until the day of Christ Jesus (Philippians 1:6).

When someone newly reborn in spirit, stands before God forgiven, pure, and clean, they are that—forgiven and new. But they must go on and live out the natural consequences of their lives—the fruits of the seeds that were lived and sown before.

When a second marriage begins, it too is a new beginning. But it brings with it much baggage from the old relationship. The children are the most obvious preexisting part of this new marriage.

Sometimes our mouths drop open when we hear a kid repeat a phrase or gesture in a way they could have gotten from nowhere except that missing parent.

When Rog and I each got married the first time, it was just two people coming together to be one. Now in our new marriage there are these children of our former oneness. They bear the physical reminders of our former love, not just in appearance, but behaviors—habits and patterns that existed with another mom and another dad. Sometimes our mouths drop open when we hear a kid repeat a phrase or gesture in a way they could have gotten from nowhere except that missing parent. I recall the double take Rog did one day, when as he was passing by the table, he caught a glimpse of a daughter's penmanship that looked identical to her deceased mother's handwriting.

These reflections of the past seen in our children are harmless enough. But the challenge is when one or both of us parents or a child expects something from the past to exist in the present that simply does not exist anymore. When I expect my husband to relate to the children exactly the same way their birthfather did, I will only be disappointed. If my husband expects me to can fruit or prepare casseroles in exactly the same way his first wife did, he will be disappointed. The children may also be disappointed when the stepparent buys computer equipment instead of sports equipment or spends more time reading and working than playing ball or playing games.

Always we are trying to blend, trying to bring the two together and make one. It is an ongoing process. After all this time we usually succeed. But sometimes still, we don't. In those times instead of blending, all we do is rub against each other's varying traditions, out-of-sync priorities, and clashing outlooks. That's when we must turn to God and plead for understanding, for wisdom, for help in accomplishing this challenging task of making one family out of two.

It has been eight years, and He has been hearing us. But I've noticed that we're really not a "blend*ed*" family." We are actually a "blend*ing*" family." The process is never quite finished. As each person in our family grows in God, as the Father does His work in each individual, so our family grows, and the blending continues. As the Christian life is a process, so is our "blending" a process—the progression of the two becoming one.

◆

Dear God, please help us to allow You to complete Your work in us. As You make us into the kind of people You want us to be, please also mold us into a family that will please You. May we give You the glory. In Jesus' name, amen.

18

No Such Thing As Instant Love

◆

Love is patient, love is kind. It does not envy, it does not boast, it is not proud.
It is not rude, it is not self-seeking, it is not easily angered, it keeps no record
of wrongs. Love does not delight in evil but rejoices with the truth. It always
protects, always trusts, always hopes, always perseveres
(1 Corinthians 13:4–7).

One of the greatest misconceptions of stepparenting is: I love my new spouse, therefore, I will automatically love his or her children. We Americans seem to have an overly romanticized sense of love, mostly believing it to be a warm, passionate feeling we helplessly "fall" into and out of at the whim of fate. In truth, love is often a conscious *decision* to be kind and committed.

Feelings change every day. When the resentment and frustrations that

When the resentment and frustrations that are quite natural to the beginning of a blended family threaten to overcome you, and you try harder and harder to pretend you have feelings of affection, the one thing left is guilt.

are quite natural to the beginning of a blended family threaten to overcome you, and you try harder and harder to pretend you have feelings of affection, the one thing left is guilt.

You feel guilty that you don't love these "innocent kids," have little compassion for their mistakes and flaws, and at times can barely stand them. According to Einstein and Albert's book, *Strengthening Your Stepfamily,* the guilt you feel for not loving your stepchild leads to more resentment (as the dream of a "perfect" family bites the dust) and might lead you to finding fault and picking on the child continually. After all, if the child is really, really bad, then you have a good reason for not loving them!

But this negative trend can be reversed if you simply don't demand an affectionate feeling from yourself or the child in the first place. Give yourselves time. Often the only person telling you that you must love this child is you. Talk with your spouse about the kids, talk about the things that are positive in each child, and as you all spend time together and purposefully nurture a friendship, feelings of love may begin to grow.

The important thing is not whether you are feeling all warm and fuzzy over your spouse's offspring; the important thing is that you are able to treat each one fairly, respectfully, and with compassion. After years of time together and this type of committed treatment, real love will grow. And it will be much better than some fuzzy, mushy, unrealistic, romantic idea of a feeling that is easily squelched for lack of sustenance.

The "instant love" myth, as Einstein and Albert call it, can set another common trap: demanding love and acceptance from a child that cannot give them.* By demanding unity where none exists, the authors warn that family members may begin to feel angry, which will lead to more resistance and rebellion against the idea of the new family and against the stepparent. The all-too-common scenario of a stepchild who hates and resents the stepparent may be erased, at least partially, if the child does not feel forced to love and accept someone they are not yet sure about.

The most happy, and at the same time most traumatic, day of our first summer together was when Becky and Lisa called me "Mommy." (I had easily become "Mom," but this was something new.) I told them it was nice to hear that name again. I explained that the boys had stopped the "mommy" in favor of "mom" the minute they started school, and I had missed it ever since.

Their older sister, Tammy, who was listening to this conversation, was not ready to refer to me in such an intimate way, and I guess she had a hard time believing her sisters could. Stricken with grief, overcome with anger, she ran screaming and crying to her room. I thank God for the wisdom He gave me on that day.

After a moment to whisper a prayer, I went to her. Sitting beside her, I told her I was never going to try to take her mother's place, that I didn't expect or want Tammy to stop loving her birthmother, but that I was simply the mom who is here right now. When I felt it was OK to do so, I stroked her hair and told her it was good to cry for her mom, and I felt sorry that she felt bad. I promised that I would take care of her and love her the best I could, but I knew it was not now and never would be "the same." But it was OK for it to not be "the same." We would live with what we had.

What stands out in my memory of that day was my own awareness that I had not yet begun to love her in a real "mommy" sort of way— like the way I loved my sons. But what I said to her gave us both permission to have a relationship that was different from that. It would be different than she had before, a relationship that didn't have to include being "mommy" unless she wanted it to.

I haven't always remembered this permission in our years together. Many times I have demanded more from our relationship than I should

50

have, causing resentment and anger in Tammy. But when I backed off, let her father parent her more, and determined only to be myself, things then became easier between my stepchild and me.

While being myself, I often think about 1 Corinthians 13 and how it tells me to act—with patience and kindness, without rudeness. After all, I can act right no matter what I "feel"! Often, with a more relaxed attitude going and acting out 1 Corinthians without thinking about "my feelings," the intimacy I was "fighting" for suddenly appears quite naturally!

◆

Thank You, Father in heaven, for being the perfect Parent, the perfect Example of love. Help us to love one another as You love us, giving our lives for each other no matter how we feel. May we always have grace to be kind. In Jesus' name, amen.

---

*Einstein and Albert, *Strengthening Your Stepfamily,* 11–13.

19
Blending Relatives

◆

Children's children are a crown to the aged, and parents are the pride of their children (Proverbs 17:6).

I have been reminded of your sincere faith, which first lived in your grandmother Lois and in your mother Eunice and, I am persuaded, now lives in you also (2 Timothy 1:5).

One of the biggest challenges to our family is staying connected to the extended family. In our case we have attempted to maintain our ties with the families of our deceased spouses. But at times this seems to be an impossible task. Just brothers and sisters-in-law number thirty-eight! And of course we have double mothers-in-law and multiple grandmas and so many aunts and uncles and cousins it took a couple of years to meet them all

We suddenly look around at Thanksgiving and realize we are having a ball with these aunts and uncles and still name-scrambled cousins with whom, finally, we have begun to share a history.

and learn their names, and some we still don't get right. Every holiday time is like a splash of cold water when Rog and I realize our children don't know their cousins the way we did growing up, and many times they can't even remember how someone is related to them. And most impossible of all is trying to visit all our grandmas as often as they would like.

But we go on, year after year. And the "someday" does come when we suddenly look around at Thanksgiving and realize we are having a ball with these aunts and uncles and still name-scrambled cousins with whom, finally, we have begun to share a history. The passage of time does that. It creates history.

Even though the holiday calendar is too full, it's worth it for all these precious, wonderful "relations" that we have worked so hard to keep in our life. And our children thrive. They have a history now of grandmas and grandpas and aunts and uncles and cousins of so many backgrounds—from Smith to DeKock.

Relatives from all four sides come to us from mission fields, sharing with us songs and lifestyles from other cultures. Some relatives come to us from nonreligious lifestyles, and we learn to hold up life and look at it in a light totally different from our own. Some are rich and some are poor. Some are not so moral as we judge morality to be, and it challenges our ability to accept the person while not loving what they do. And many of the lives that are part of us are varying shades of the same color life we live.

But all of these people are, if we let them, part of our family now, our blended family. They are parts of the whole that make this new group who we are, and we are the richer for it.

◆

Dear God and Father of us all, we thank You for the diversity of our children's relatives. We pray that You will help us to view our multiple parents, grandparents, in-law siblings, aunts, uncles, and cousins as the rich blessing that they are and not as a burden. We thank You that we are able to love all of them with love from You, which is more perfect than any love we could manufacture on our own. In Jesus' name, amen.

20

When the Extended Family
Does Not Accept the New Spouse

◆

*Do not repay anyone evil for evil. . . . Do not take revenge, my friends, . . . If
your enemy is hungry, feed him; if he is thirsty, give him something to drink.
In doing this, you will heap burning coals on his head. Do not be overcome by
evil, but overcome evil with good (Romans 12:17b, 19a, 20–21).*

In doing this, you will heap burning coals on his head, and the LORD *will
reward you (Proverbs 25:22).*

My friend Janice, a young wife with two school-age children, had never been accepted by her mother-in-law. The mother-in-law didn't believe in divorce. Like a dreamy-eyed child, she kept hoping her son and his first wife would get back together. It didn't matter to her that the first marriage was a teenage mistake in judgment, that it lasted only briefly, and that there were no children. She didn't care that her son, Jim, had established a new life with Janice and had children with her. In this

After years of trying to guess what would make them happy and often guessing wrong, after acting first one way and then another in response to their inconsistencies and trying to please them, I decided to follow one plan: "Kill 'em with kindness."

mother's mind Jim belonged with his first wife and that was that.

With great pain Janice realized that she and her children probably never would be accepted by her husband's family. The question then became, How should she and her husband treat his mother?

The truth is, my friend cannot change her mother-in-law. Neither she nor her husband can force his mother to accept their marriage. But the verse above offers some sound advice. The footnote in my New International Version of the Bible explains that carrying coals on one's head was an Egyptian expiation ritual in which a guilty person, as a sign of repentance, carried a basin of hot coals on his or her head. The meaning here is that in returning good for evil, you may cause the other person to repent or change. Doing good to one's "enemy," instead of trying to take revenge, may bring about repentance or the changing of his or her mind. But the end of the verse in Proverbs assures, even if the enemy does not repent, "the LORD will reward you."

So what Janice can do is remain pleasant. On holidays she can remember the difficult parent with notes and cards or maybe even send flowers or some other deliverable item.

She and Jim can try to compensate for their children's loss by enjoying her parents and relatives. By establishing sound relationships on that side of the family, they can give their children a sense of continuity and belonging. They may even adopt an elderly neighbor or friend as a "grandma substitute."

I've had to cope, long-term, with people who rejected me—people I could never please but for some unavoidable reason were a permanent fixture in my life. After years of trying to guess what would make them happy and often guessing wrong, after acting first one way and then another in response to their inconsistencies, I decided to follow one plan: "Kill 'em with kindness."

This is actually what the verse above means, and it works! By following the advice of Scripture, I no longer had to struggle with questions like, "What do they want from me?" "How did I go wrong this time?" "What will please them next time?" I had a plan to follow and I would always act the same, no matter what they did or said.

Before each encounter with my difficult person, it became very worthwhile for me to fill up on encouragement from God's Word and to say a prayer for strength and stability. I then had the security of knowing that whatever mood my difficult person was in, I would know how I was going to act and what I was going to do.

Today I have a pleasant relationship with my difficult person—but it only came after I no longer cared whether it happened or not. When I decided always to act the same toward her, no matter what she did or said, I was rewarded as Proverbs says, with "the repentance" of my enemy. At first my reward was simply the peace I acquired from ceasing to worry about it so much. The actual repentance of my "enemy" was just an extra benefit of acting the way God wanted me to act.

◆

Dear Lord Jesus, please be with me each time I must encounter the difficult persons of my life. Help me to act as You would want me to act and not worry about pleasing them. In Your name and for Your glory I pray, amen.

21

When the Children Are
Not Accepted by Grandparents

◆

Commit your way to the LORD; trust in him and he will do this: He will make your righteousness shine like the dawn, the justice of your cause like the noonday sun. Be still before the LORD and wait patiently for him; do not fret when men succeed in their ways, when they carry out their wicked schemes. Refrain from anger and turn from wrath; do not fret—it leads only to evil. For evil men will be cut off, but those who hope in the LORD will inherit the land (Psalm 37:5–9).

It is very painful when grandparents don't accept the stepchildren as their grandchildren. I have heard all kinds of horror stories about this rejection. The worst case, of course, is at a family Christmas celebration when the grandparents give expensive gifts or big checks to their "real" grandchildren and only token gifts or nothing at all to the stepgrandchildren. You hurt because your children are hurt, and

You hurt because your children are hurt, and your happy and blessed holiday turns into a pain-filled experience from which you would all rather escape.

your happy and blessed holiday turns into a pain-filled experience from which you would all rather escape.

As with most other adjustments in this blended-family story, talk, talk, talk is the answer. A spouse may have to talk to his or her parents and set limits with them, explain that you are a family now and you would like all children to be treated the same. Perhaps they can be persuaded to spend less on your birthchildren so the same amount of money for gifts can be divided among all of the children. Or you can have your Christmas celebration with those grandparents when the other children are with their other parent. While one set of children is getting gifts from the one parent's side of the family, the other set of children can be getting gifts from another side. Or in situations over which no amount of planning and discussion will avail, you may have to simply make up the difference yourself by bringing along your own gifts for the slighted children.

Talk to the children. Find out how much they care and what they expect. Children who have things explained to them both before and after a situation may amaze their parents with their own sensitivity and ability to understand.

We have some wonderful grandmas who from day one have treated all of our children the same. Their "real" grandchildren and the new children in the family all receive the same amount of gifts and attention. I know that God will bless them and reward them many times over for the love and acceptance they have shown to us.

We have another grandparent who did not really want to be a grandparent to the stepchildren. This relative would take a set of kids out for their birthdays but never even ask when the birthdays occurred for the stepchildren. Miraculously, this situation balanced out well when an aunt from another side of the family very generously asked if she could take our children out for their birthdays. With thankful hearts we explained our situation and asked that she only take out the kids who were slighted by the grandparent. So as the years flow by, all of our children have a relative who takes them out to lunch on their birthdays, and it doesn't matter at all that it's not the same relative.

The emotion of these inequities can be minimized, as I said, by discussing them with the children. Explain (if you can) the nature and point of view of the grandparent. Some people are not malicious, just simply insensitive or small minded. Of course, some are malicious, but even that painful truth can be talked about. "Nannie is not kind to everyone because she is angry about . . ."

Never assume that people are feeling bad, and never assume that things are OK. Do a "feelings check-up" with your kids and spouse, and make sure that what is happening during visits with grandparents is really OK with them all.

In all the talking to the parents, grandparents, and kids, don't forget to talk to God. He promises in the first chapter of James to give wisdom generously to all who ask. So do ask.

———————◆———————

Dear God, our Protector and Comforter, we thank You that You have not asked us to face any pain or struggle alone. Thank You that You are there, and as Your Word says, You give wisdom to those who ask. Thank You that You care more about our children and our family than even we do.
In Your Son's name we pray, amen.

22
True Coparenting

◆

Do not think of yourself more highly than you ought, but rather think of yourself with sober judgment, in accordance with the measure of faith God has given you. . . . We have different gifts, according to the grace given us (Romans 12:3b, 6a).

A contemporary author of Christian self-help books challenges readers to ask themselves if they will get their sense of worth from what others think or from what God's Word says.* This question has become very important to my outlook on life, for there are many untrustworthy judges of me as a stepmom—not the least of which are the

> *I have also discovered that when he has had time to think, my husband comes up with some very creative ways to make the discipline fit the "crime."*

children. For example, in her anger my stepdaughter blames me—the wicked stepmother—for her problems. I am hurt and angry. And even as one part of my brain knows this particular problem cannot possibly be "my fault," there is a guilty little voice somewhere telling me that it is—"It is always the mother's responsibility how the children turn out, is it not?"

Of course that voice is not true. But my own guilt, no matter how illogical, accuses me a lot more often as a stepmother than it does as a mother. There is a difference in how I think my flaws will affect the children. No matter how irrational it is, I think my parenting mistakes will harm my stepdaughters more than my sons.

We often hear that God has "loaned us" our children to raise for Him. With my stepdaughters, I find myself thinking they have been loaned to me from God and their birthmother. So despite the fact that she's not alive, there are times when I feel accountable to her or, if not accountable to her specifically, just more accountable. I have a feeling of nervous insecurity about whether or not I am doing the right thing much more often regarding the girls than the boys.

But the truth is God has brought all of us together because He knew we would be best for each other. I must think of myself with "sober judgment." I must think reasonably, think seriously, evaluate myself with sound thinking—not hysterical thinking! I have a tendency to take responsibility where it is not due. I must remind myself that I answer to God and to my husband for how I raise the children. I do not answer to an absent parent or any other relative, living or dead. I may have to say this to myself hundreds of times to get my feelings in line, but it is the truth.

Being so acutely aware of our accountability to God and each other for "someone else's children," however, has resulted in an obvious good in our home. I charge ahead by myself less often and am more likely to deal with issues only after more thinking and input from the children's father. We both know how sensitive an area it is—this parenting each other's children. So more often than we probably did with the birthparents, we talk things over with each other.

When I feel burdened with those daily decisions that need to be made regarding the children (all the children), I find myself calling my husband's office and leaving messages on voice mail for him. When he gets home, he already knows what's going on with the kids—both the boys and the girls—and has had time to think over all of it. I may have begun this practice because I felt accountable to him for his children, but as I continue to do it, I find the pleasant result is we coparent a lot more. I much prefer this type of parenting to "everything being up to me"!

I have also discovered that when he has had time to think, my husband comes up with some very creative ways to make the discipline fit the "crime." I'll never forget the day I called him because Aaron had once again taken off on his bike without telling me where he was going. I said to Rog, "I just don't think a spanking will work this time, but what can we do?" When Rog came home from work, he stayed outside for a few extra minutes to implement his carefully-thought-out plan. He chained Aaron's bike up in the front of the garage, a place the erring child would see it every day. But as Rog had the key, it would be inaccessible for two weeks. Needless to say, Aaron never took off on that bike again without first checking with one of us!

Combining Rog's problem-solving skills and creative discipline with my abilities to identify the problem and "patch up" the hurting make us a good parenting team. But we are a team only when we both enter into the raising of each other's children, and that means being in communication concerning all of the children all of the time.

What started out as my irrational guilt led to the positive experience of both of us being totally involved with all of the children. We all became the winners when Rog and I learned to think "with sound judgment" and use our own specific gifts. Now I can think of myself more reasonably because I have freed myself from false responsibility (guilt) and moved to shared responsibility (a truly two-parent home). And as usual, the winners are both the children and our relationship.

———————◆———————

Dear Jesus, thank You that You thought I was worth so much You died for me. Help me remember how much I am worth as Your child. Yes, I am different from the children's birthmother, but you made me who I am. Help me be the best me I can be in their lives. In Jesus' name, amen.

———————

*Dr. Chris Thurman, *The Lies We Believe* (Nashville: Nelson, 1989), 42–45.

23
Winning Over the Nonaccepting Child

◆

*I can do all things through Christ which strengtheneth me
(Philippians 4:13 KJV).*

*But he said to me, "My grace is sufficient for you, for my power is made
perfect in weakness" (2 Corinthians 12:9).*

*I pray that out of his glorious riches he may strengthen you with power
through his Spirit in your inner being (Ephesians 3:16).*

My friend Roxie had a hard time winning over the children of her new husband, Rob. Her kids were already teens, and his, of whom he had custody, were still in early elementary school. They moved into her house, and she felt invaded—not to mention overwhelmed—by all the work and mess created by a sudden addition of four people!

They noticed that the better their marriage relationship, the better the stepparent's relationship with the children.

Because she wanted his children to be responsible and do the things around the house she had taught her children to do when they were that age, she found herself "on their case." They were young, but she knew what they could do as far as picking up after themselves and helping with chores. But they had not been doing these things before the marriage, and the children resented her for trying to teach them to do them now.

It got so bad that one of the children would not talk to her or even look at her. You can imagine the strain that this put on the marriage! Roxie often felt hopeless and at the end of her rope.

She finally decided to "start from scratch" with the children. One of the things she had usually done, but now she made a special point of doing every day, was really listen to each child when they had something to say. Now this may not sound like a big deal, but when you have nine people in one house and such a variety of ages, it is very challenging for the mom to "mother" on such diverse levels. Despite the difficulties, she attempted to draw each child out and really take an interest in his or her day.

Besides the personal interest, she also decided to back off on all instruction and discipline. She determined to go to her husband for every single item and let him, with her present, instruct the child or discipline the child. They tried "wait 'til your father gets home" with all of his children. Although this plan was often impractical and always challenging, it presented a united front to the kids. Now it was not just "Roxie being mean" or "Roxie being strict," this was "Dad and Mom want you to learn to do this" or "We believe that you have done wrong and this will be your punishment."

It was a touching and rewarding day when Rob's youngest child began to call her "mom." Yes, this youngster has another mom too, for her birthmother is in the picture. But Roxie is the mom of this house, and when the child is there, she calls her "mom." The other two children have not gone so far as to name her their mom, but there is no more refusing to acknowledge her. They now have a workable relationship.

Obviously, this took a tremendous amount of effort, self-discipline, time, and a willingness to keep at it. Winning over the nonaccepting child is definitely not something that happens automatically or overnight. But as can be seen by this very difficult situation, improvements can be made.

I cannot leave out the fact that during this struggle Roxie and Rob began to have devotions together. They had not done this before, and in addition to their own prayers, they asked a group of friends to pray for them. Reading the Bible together led them to discuss things better than they ever had, and prayer released the power of God into their lives. As their marriage relationship was strengthened, so was their blended family. They noticed that the better their marriage relationship, the better the stepparent's relationship with the children.

◆

Dear Father in heaven, thank You that when we are not wise enough or strong enough or patient enough, You can give us strength and power from Your Spirit. Thank You for Your Word, from which we can get wisdom, and for prayer, through which we can be empowered in our inner being. Thank You that we are not stepparenting alone, but that You are there, if we only call out to You. In the power of Jesus' name we pray, amen.

24

Needed: Wise Counsel to Win the Nonaccepting Child

◆

I look but there is no one—no one among them to give counsel, no one to give answer when I ask them (Isaiah 41:28).

Let the wise listen and add to their learning, and let the discerning get guidance (Proverbs 1:5).

For waging war you need guidance, and for victory many advisers (Proverbs 24:6).

The biggest, most immediate challenge for any blended family is whether or not the children will accept their mom or dad's new spouse. Even if they got along great during the courtship, it is not an automatic given that the children—or a certain child—will

> *The "honeymoon stage" for the kids is definitely over as soon as the family begins living together.*

continue this camaraderie into living together. The "honeymoon stage" for the kids is definitely over as soon as the family begins living together. Even very nice children may do things they have never done before as they struggle with letting go of the old family and attempt to accept the stepparent and the new family. At times it feels like a war, but it's a war the family must win.

I have already mentioned my sense of false accountability and fear that I might "damage" my stepchildren with my parenting mistakes. So imagine the sense of isolation and frustration I experienced when no one, no friends of the family, no relatives who knew my stepchildren, not even my husband, could believe a sweet child would do what I insisted one of the stepchildren was doing to me!

I began to question my own sanity. Could I really be so insecure that I imagined it all? This situation became the occasion for our first counseling with a professional. And we found that it was not my imagination! Of course the child was doing and saying things she had never done before; she had never had a stepmother before!

She wanted to preserve a past that was no longer there. Saying things like, "You're breaking those dishes on purpose because you don't care about them" or "My mom never cooked it that way, I won't eat it" or "What are you doing to 'my' house?" were a result of her very natural longing to get back the life she had lost.

The counselor helped her to let go of the past and gave her the permission she needed to love and accept me. I learned to remind her that I was not the same as her birthmom and I knew I could never take her mother's place. But I was there to love her and care for her, a different mom—a stepmom—the mom of this house. I'm simply the mom God has put in this home, and she is the daughter I "get" to be the mom to.

In my prayers beside each child's bed at night, I began to say, "Thank You, Lord, that I get to be the mom of _____," a simple statement that helped to turn the burden of responsibility and adjustment into a privilege. But this was a privileged responsibility that I could not understand or respond to correctly until I got the counsel of someone who understood the child and the situation of blending families much more than I did.

At times for us, and unfortunately for many others, attempts to blend a family do seem much like waging a war. I know of a very sad second marriage that never succeeded in becoming a blended family. It is the tragic tale of Karen, a stepmom who never was able to work it out with her stepdaughters. Heather was a teen and Hillary was early elementary age when they formed their new family. Like us, both parents were widowed. Karen and David were so happy and excited about finding each other and once again being a "whole" family that they formally adopted each other's children. But though blended on paper, they never made it to being "one."

It all started out just like ours—friction between the oldest daughter and the new mom. When Heather said mean, judgmental, or rejecting things to Karen, she internalized the comments and often believed the bad stuff. The younger stepdaughter, who could very well have bonded with this kind and nurturing woman, shared a room with her older sister and listened day after day to the criticism and complaints. Eventually Hillary too, out of loyalty to her sister, began the habit of continual ridicule of the stepmother, rejecting Karen's attempts to bond and refusing to cooperate.

Karen did get counseling. But leery of "professionals," she sought out a person who, though a very nice pastor, was not trained for this kind of situation and knew nothing about blended families or stepparenting. Patching her up with spiritual platitudes was of no help. She needed trained intervention.

As the level of anger and frustration mounted, the hostility and division in their home grew, until they finally ended up living as two hostile camps in one house, the father in the middle, the mother and stepdaughters forever on opposing sides. This is the point at which many would divorce. Although they did not choose to divorce, they have lived in a divided house as angry and bitter people.

There is "safety in a multitude of counselors," and I cannot say enough about getting help, getting the right kind of help, and getting that help before irreparable damage has been done to the family. Many Christian counseling organizations have fees based on ability to pay. Please do not allow the cost to be a hindrance. Get the help you need. It could be worth the life of your family. And if the first counselor is not helpful, try again.

Use whatever outside help you need to turn the war-torn family into a united family. Though the seam in a blended family will always show, with the help of God and "many counselors," you can truly blend.

◆

Dear Lord, thank You that I did not have to remain isolated, without counsel and understanding. Thank You for wise, well-trained, effective counselors and what they have meant to the blending of this family and to many others who struggle. Thank You for Your Spirit that led us to them. We glorify You for all You have done for us. In Jesus' name, amen.

25
When to Get Help

◆

Praise be to the God and Father of our Lord Jesus Christ, the Father of compassion and the God of all comfort, who comforts us in all our troubles, so that we can comfort those in any trouble with the comfort we ourselves have received from God. For just as the sufferings of Christ flow over into our lives, so also through Christ our comfort overflows (2 Corinthians 1:3–5).

My friend Susan entered her second marriage just at the time I was entering my first. Her marriage started out as a beautiful love story—of how God took two broken and lonely hearts and made them heal with each other. But the love and affection between them was not enough to overcome the problems presented by his oldest daughter, Cari, and the birthmother's parents.

If you ever get to the place where you feel you really need help and all your friends say you don't need it, don't listen! Get help anyway.

My friend could not discipline Cari without a tirade from the deceased mother's parents. Having never really accepted the loss of their daughter, they refused to think of their son-in-law's new wife as anything but a scoundrel. They accused her of everything a wicked stepmother is thought to be, as if the fairy tales were true and she really was going to roast her stepchild in an oven and eat her!

In all her selfish, childish wisdom, Cari continued to carry tales—exaggerated or out of context—to her grandparents who always took her side. They babied their grandchild and bullied Susan until there was so much antagonism that the now teenaged girl had to leave her father's house. Those misguided grandparents would not let their granddaughter have them and her family too! The sad young girl lost not only the stepmother she was trying to lose but also her father and siblings.

The key here could have been Pete, the father. But he, fond of his former in-laws and unwilling to confront either his daughter or her grandparents, chose to avoid it all, unfortunately leaving Susan to cope as best she could. Pete found it an impossible situation, but he did not seek help.

Susan determined help was needed. But when she sought referrals and support from friends, well-meaning people told her she was doing a great job and with all her insight, things were sure to get better. Even her pastor told her she was doing a wonderful job and not to worry, the problems would pass. Unfortunately, she listened to them. When she finally got help, Susan and Pete had already lost Cari.

After Cari left, they did seek counseling and began to build a tenuous relationship with her again. Susan has now been in therapy for years. The insight she gained with professional help, combined with the wisdom she attained from growing in the Lord, has helped her understand what happened. But sadly, nothing can undo it.

Her story is so sad, why do I tell it? I must tell her story because it was her words and the story of her life that echoed in my mind and made me brave enough to make that first call for help.

She said to me, "If you ever get to the place where you feel you really need help and all your friends say you don't need it, don't listen! Get help anyway." And her life sadly illustrated the truth of her point. In her pain she was able to give me the best advice anyone ever offered to me on how to blend our family, for in "getting help" we began to really heal and to blend.

◆

Dear Jesus, thank You for my friend Susan. Thank You that she was willing to share her pain, and in that sharing, I found the fortitude I needed to get help. Thank You that You brought her words to me at just the right time. In Jesus' name, amen.

26
Restoration of Broken Relationships

◆

"Even now," declares the LORD, "return to me with all your heart, with fasting and weeping and mourning." Rend your heart and not your garments. Return to the LORD your God, for he is gracious and compassionate, slow to anger and abounding in love, and he relents from sending calamity. Who knows? He may turn and have pity and leave behind a blessing (Joel 2:12–14a).

"I will repay you for the years the locusts have eaten . . . and you will praise the name of the LORD your God, who has worked wonders for you; never again will my people be shamed. Then you will know that I am in Israel, that I am the LORD your God, and that there is no other (Joel 2:25a, 26b, 27a).

I cannot tell the story in devotion 25 without saying that Susan has seen miracles of God in her life. Years of fervent prayer, combined with counseling and reaching out in love, have restored to her a relationship with her stepdaughter. They still walk carefully with one another so as to avoid pain. But with forgiveness, hard work, and commitment, they have built a relationship tailored just for them. And they give God the glory.

> *But one of the most prevailing reasons they feel they cannot repair what they call "a sham of a marriage" is what seems to be a total inability to forgive on both their parts.*

I have seen marriages restored, stepparents and stepchildren blend when it seemed futile and hopeless, and marriages miraculously preserved when living out God's call to forgive and be forgiven.

We have known Ron and Phyllis, parents in a blended family, for years, and they have just about called it quits on their marriage. They have reached this stage for many reasons, some of which go all the way back to their childhoods. But the prevailing reason they feel they cannot repair what they call "a sham of a marriage" is the total inability of both to forgive.

"He said that" but "She said that so we're even" are messages sent between them all the time. Stuff is said and jabs are given, and all the wrongs are tallied and scores kept until it seems there is no hope of ever getting to the bottom of their troubles, let alone fixing them. Several times Phyllis has tried to start over with the help of counseling, but Ron hasn't been willing to take the risk and change his behavior. Now he is willing to try a few things, but she feels the hurting has gone on so long that she is no longer willing to forgive him enough to accept the new things he tries. If their marriage ever is to succeed, they both must learn to forgive, and they haven't quite arrived at that place.

The scariest thing about this troubled marriage is that most all the hurt each of them talk about is just like your hurt or my hurt or the hurt that occurs in any marriage. The difference is that in their unforgiveness, they have allowed the downward cycle of hostility and pain to go on, growing larger and larger until it has just about consumed their relationship.

The things Ron and Phyllis do to each other have all been done before. But their inability to forgive, combined with continually making wrong choices, has placed them in a mode of total failure. In the beginning it started out like any other struggling, adjusting relationship. Now, spinning way out of control, their marriage is fueled with bitterness and rage, a lack of obedience to the Word of God, and a total unwillingness to forgive.

If they would throw away their stubborn pride, "rend their hearts instead of their garments" (a middle-eastern expression of extreme grief), and fall on their faces asking forgiveness of God and each other, God would hear their cry for mercy, restore their souls, and restore their marriage.

If my friend Susan and her stepdaughter can come to a workable relationship after their years of alienation and pain, if Rob and Roxie can miraculously learn to have a relationship when they didn't know how, then these desperate friends can restore their marriage. But only if they learn to forgive.

———————◆———————

Dear God in heaven, thank You for teaching us how to love each other. Thank You for the counselor that showed us how to get out of our cycle of pain and anger and go on to renewed love and joy. Please empower, dear Holy Spirit, Your children who need to forgive. Teach them to forgive one another as You have forgiven them. In the powerful name of Jesus we pray, amen.

27
The Depressed Child

◆

An anxious heart weighs a man down, but a kind word cheers him up
(Proverbs 12:25).

Therefore, as God's chosen people, holy and dearly loved, clothe yourselves with
compassion, kindness, humility, gentleness and patience (Colossians 3:12).

I have written about getting help for the unaccepting, angry child—counseling for both the stepparents and stepchildren to enable them to get along. Another major reason you may need to get professional help for your child or stepchild is for depression.

A stepfamily is built from the loss of the nuclear family.

A stepfamily is built from the loss of the nuclear family. Whether by death or divorce, the first marriage has ended and so has the day-to-day involvement of a birthparent in the lives of the children. The end of this involvement, even if it was a negative involvement, represents a loss in the child's life, and this loss can be a cause for depression.

It is possible that a child may not have a particularly difficult time accepting his stepparent and doesn't particularly seem to mind the new living arrangements, but there still seems to be something amiss. At first it may be easy to ignore the problem of depression in a child who, rather than lashing out in anger, chooses to quietly withdraw from the family.

But stepparents beware—depressed children may manifest their symptoms in many ways. Overt anger is one of them—but so is suddenly doing poorly in school, becoming excessively clingy, compulsively overeating or refusing to eat almost at all, and withdrawing from friends and family. I know a family where petty stealing, lying, constant irritability, and difficulty concentrating (where these things did not exist before) were signals of a depressed and troubled child.

According to Dr. Richard Gardner, the above are all signs of depression in children. In severe cases, depressed children may become preoccupied with self-destructive fantasies, accident prone, and unconcerned for their personal safety. If your child exhibits any of these signs, get help.*

You can help your children by reaching out to them in love, kindness, and compassion. Be there for your children; make attempts at drawing them out, listening, or simply engaging in activities with them.

Bonnie and David Juroe, counselors, authors, and themselves stepparents, recommend that you guard against having your stepchild withdraw from everyone and everything. Filling up his or her days with many activities so that he or she won't have time to dwell on negative thoughts is good therapy. They also quote an old proverb which says, "It's easier to act yourself into a new way of feeling than to feel yourself into a new way of acting."

As you help your stepchild plan activities and outings or simply become involved in school or church, you can create a spirit of excitement and anticipation. The Juroes say, "All the time he is planning and anticipating, he is getting his mind off his past hurts."[†]

So parents beware. The difficult child who makes the most noise, who causes the most upheaval in the home, may not be the only one that needs special help and attention. Watch for signs of depression in your children, attempt to love them out of it, and get help when it is needed.

———————◆———————

Dear Lord, please make me very sensitive and wise as I learn to know my stepchildren. Please help me to reach out in love and compassion to them and treat them with gentleness and patience. Love them through me, and love away their hurt. In Jesus' name I pray, amen.

*Richard Gardner, *The Parent's Book About Divorce* (Garden City, N.Y.: Doubleday, 1977), 200.

†David J. and Bonnie B. Juroe, *Successful Stepparenting* (Old Tappan, N.J.: Power Books, 1983), 48.

28

Acceptance by Friends

◆

Bear with each other and forgive whatever grievances you may have against one another. Forgive as the Lord forgave you (Colossians 3:13).

"But I tell you who hear me: Love your enemies, do good to those who hate you, bless those who curse you, pray for those who mistreat you" (Luke 6:27–28).

And you also are among those who are called to belong to Jesus Christ (Romans 1:6).

In our first days together, some of my husband's first wife's friends wanted to be my friends too, and I was willing. Naively I accepted overtures of friendship that proved, in some cases, to have the ulterior motive of fulfilling a need for control over our family. Part of us had been part of their lives, and in their grief over the departed one, they wanted to hang on to our family.

Naively I accepted overtures of friendship that proved, in some cases, to have the ulterior motive of fulfilling a need for control over our family.

They were not seeking my *personal* friendship but were calling me and making offers of friendship so they could make sure everything was "OK" with the part of our family they cared about. And if they didn't think it was OK (interpretation: if it's not the way it used to be), I found myself a target of criticism and catty remarks.

Before I understood the nature of these relationships and because I struggled with a certain child, I shared my concern with an apparent friend or two because they had known the child longer than I had. I thought these friends were safe and accepted me and my struggles. They, however, thought I was awful and unloving for thinking that this precious, innocent child, in whom they never observed a problem, could really be creating a problem for me. (Of course the child never did anything like this before—he or she never had a stepmother before!)

I wrote the following to a fellow stepmother friend:

"And on top of all this stuff from the kid—there are those gossipy women—so smug in their own little nuclear families—who don't understand at all about 'stepmother' and so everybody thinks I'm bad and face it—they might be right?!"

But God said to me, "I called you by name [stepmother]; you are mine" (Isaiah 43:1–3).

I am a stepmother. I am my husband's second wife. I am not just like his first wife; I am not the same kind of mother she was, but that doesn't make me bad or wrong.

Gradually I learned to be more cautious about relationships and to admit that it might not be healthy for me to be friends with everyone who offers a relationship. As an imager of Christ, I will attempt to forgive, love, and accept people as well as I can; but acceptance does not mean that I can be close friends with everyone.

◆

Dear Father, thank You that from Your example and by Your power I can learn real forgiveness. Help me to evaluate myself according to Your Word and not according to anyone else's judgment. Thank You that You care for me and are involved in all of my life, even my friendships. In Jesus' name, amen.

29
Knowing Each Other Through the Company You Keep

◆

By this all men will know that you are my disciples, if you have love for one another (John 13:35).

A friend loves at all times (Proverbs 17:17a).

Do not forsake your friend (Proverbs 27:10a).

I thank my God every time I remember you. In all my prayers for all of you, I always pray with joy because of your partnership in the gospel from the first day until now (Philippians 1:3–5).

The difficulty of being accepted by someone else's social group is by no means only a female problem, but in our situation, I was the one who had moved into Rog's neighborhood, church, and school. Rog's experience was quite different from mine.

When he met me, I was recently transplanted from Florida to Michigan. My extended family lived in Michigan, but since I had been in Florida more than six years, my friends had scattered to the far winds

He felt, he says, as if this group of warm and loving Christians could be picked up and transported right into the middle of our church fellowship hall back in Michigan, and the scene would continue unchanged.

and there wasn't a convenient way for Rog to get to know the people that used to be close to me. My friends hadn't forsaken me; they had just moved to new neighborhoods, joined different churches, worked in other places. There was no place in Michigan I could take Rog and say, "These are my friends." Oh sure, they all came together for the wedding, but what can you tell about a person's friends in two minutes of social gab at a wedding reception?

People are partly defined by the company they keep (John 13:35), and unbeknown to me, my new husband had an unsettled feeling— sometimes an actual sense of fear—that he didn't really know this woman he had married because he didn't really know many of her friends! But all of this didn't last long.

We had honeymooned after our wedding in March, but in June, when the kids were out of school, we went on a "family honeymoon" to Florida. This was where I had just come from a year and a half before, and this was where my two boys had grown into elementary-school youngsters. This was where I had had two serious operations and faced my husband's death—all with the love and support of wonderful, dedicated friends who were still there. So off we went to meet the friends that had, as the Scripture says, loved us through all kinds of times.

Rog says that the day he walked into the park in Pompano Beach and mingled with my old friends, the members of my former social group, a great sense of relief flooded him. He felt, he says, as if this group of warm and loving Christians could be picked up and transported right into the middle of our church fellowship hall back in Michigan, and the scene would continue unchanged. No, they weren't a group of Dutch people! But they were mostly well educated, mostly family oriented, mostly from humble origins, and most of all, brothers and sisters in the family of God. He felt like he was really seeing who I was.

As I look back on this time, I realize that all Rog needed to do was *tell* me he wanted to meet more of my friends, and I could have tried harder to bring them together. We could have postponed the wedding another month or two to give him this time to feel more confident about this missing part of me. But our children and our extended families were our primary focus, taking most of our time and energy not only for our entire courtship, but also for the first two or three years of our marriage.

As the years have unfolded, however, we have both found our places with the old friends who are part of who we were. We have learned who fits into our lives now and what couples go best with our new "coupleness." We have found our places in each other's social groups, and in those groups, we have learned to know each other better too.

————◆————

Dear Father in Heaven, thank You for friends, not only people who are there for us when we need them, but who are also part of who and what we are. Thank You for how we can know one another better and grow together as we mingle with other people—our friends. In Jesus' name, amen.

30
Coping with the "Ex"

◆

Jesus replied, "No one who puts his hand to the plow and looks back is fit for service in the kingdom of God" (Luke 9:62).

. . . for he [God] has said, "I will never leave you or forsake you." So we can say with confidence, "The Lord is my helper; I will not be afraid. What can anyone do to me?" (Hebrews 13:5b–6 NRSV).

Nine of us sat around a table sharing a meal, our family— my husband, our two sons, and me—and the family of our host—Cliff, his wife, Ann, and the three children which are his from a previous marriage. The pie was just being served when the telephone rang. Cliff answered.

"Yes. Yes. OK. Bye." He turned to his wife and said, "That was the childrens' mother; she's ready for me to take them home now."

As he made a move to leave, his pie half eaten, his guests—us—still

He could not control the decisions she made at that time, and he cannot control his ex-wife now. But he can choose, to some degree, the power she exerts in his new life. He can choose to stop being afraid of what she will do.

at the table, Ann asked, "Aren't you going to finish dessert? Why does it have to be right this instant? Please," she kindly pleaded, "sit down and finish. Wait until our guests leave." In the meantime, the children scuffled to get ready to go, assuming it did mean "right this instant."

Cliff waited, but all the while he was uncomfortable and nervous. He had allowed his ex-wife to maintain unreasonable power over his life because, after all, she is attached to the children. He feared that at her slightest whim she might steal away his children again and challenge the fragile harmony of their weekend visitations. She alone had the power to further limit the children's time in his life.

The courts are not so biased for the mother now as they were when his sad case was tried. This man was devastated by divorce. He still feels the trauma of that horrendous day when, forced by legal mandate, he had to get into his car and drive away from the home he built and the children he loved.

His responsibility to them would not end as he would continue to pay for that home and their support. But from that moment he would no longer be allowed to live there and participate in their day-to-day lives because his wife had chosen another man. He could not control the decisions she made at that time, and he cannot control his ex-wife now. But he can choose, to some degree, the power she exerts in his new life. He can choose to stop being afraid of what she will do.

Talking to a good lawyer and becoming more confident of his visitation rights has helped. And coming to understand that although his ex-wife may have initiated a nightmare he wanted no part of, now he does have a life and a new marriage, and she cannot rule in it.

It has taken some time, some counseling, and a lot of patience on Ann's part, but he has learned to quit being afraid of what his "ex" might do.

◆

Dear Sovereign God, so many times we do not understand why it seems You are silent while evil strikes in the lives of Your children. But we affirm now our belief that You have a plan, that You are always there, and that You care. Thank You that You promise never to leave us or forsake us. In the sure name of Jesus we pray, amen.

31
Haunted by the First Wife

◆

For we are God's workmanship, created in Christ Jesus to do good works, which God prepared in advance for us to do (Ephesians 2:10).

Perseverance must finish its work so that you may be mature and complete (James 1:4a).

Living ex-spouses are not the only kind of former spouses that cause competition.

"What's wrong with you?" my husband pleaded one day. "Why are you so silent? I can tell you are angry! Talk to me! Tell me what you want."

> But what does he think of me in comparison to her?

"I can't."

"Why not?"

"Because," came my sheepish reply, "I'm trying to be more quiet and submissive—like your first wife." (The unspoken message: "So you'll like me better.")

"You've got to be kidding! For Pete's sake! I married you because you are the way you are! Of course I don't like getting yelled at. But I don't want you to be quiet like this. I married an outgoing woman and that's what I expect. Besides," he grinned, "this is impossible for you, isn't it?"

And as I nodded in agreement, we burst out laughing. With the tension released, I could tell him what was wrong. And I promised to try to only be myself. (Hopefully, the best self I can be—but for sure—ME.)

But what does Rog think of me in comparison to her, his first wife? I admit to thinking like this in the beginning of our marriage. "If I try to be more like her, will we get along better?" I tried it. And of course it was very foolish of me.

In all honesty, I think about both of my husbands sometimes, and I know that Rog thinks about both of his wives. But in our minds it truly is not a "he's better than him" or "she's better than her" sort of thing. Although I am sure we each have things in common with our spouse's first mate (both of my husbands have nearly identical handwriting!), we experience each other now in such totally different ways that our former marriages are not comparable to this marriage. It would be like

78

comparing Florida with Michigan. There are some absolutely wonderful things about both places, things that are totally unlike one another. And there are some undesirable things about each that are totally unlike as well. And there are some things that are remarkably similar. I loved and accepted my first husband, and now I am loving and accepting my second husband in the same way that he totally loves and accepts me.

But at the beginning of our relationship, in moments of insecurity, in times of stress and unhappiness as we tried to find our own unique coupleness, we sometimes tried to be what we were not. In attempting to please each other, at a time when we didn't know each other well enough, we tried to be someone else with characteristics we could only guess the other would like. But when those characteristics are not who we really are—it doesn't work. And while there will always be things about both of us that need refinement in the fire of God's power, we are two special individuals whom God put together. We are together because we felt it would bring glory to God, and now we have to be the special and unique individuals God wants us to be—building our own coupleness.

◆

Dear Lord, please be Lord of my life. Help me to be totally the person you
have in mind for me. May I always be growing in mind and spirit,
building into myself more each day that character that would please you.
In Jesus' name, amen.

32

My Children Are Part of a Family That Doesn't Include Me

◆

For the LORD your God is a merciful God; he will not abandon or destroy you (Deuteronomy 4:31a).

Can a mother forget the baby at her breast and have no compassion on the child she has borne? Though she may forget, I will not forget you! See, I have engraved you on the palms of my hands (Isaiah 49:15–16a).

Casting all your care upon Him; for He careth for you (1 Peter 5:7 KJV).

Once upon a time John and Fran divorced. It was as painful and as difficult as those things can be; but after quite awhile, acceptance and healing were reached. The children grew accustomed to every-other weekend with their father, a week at spring break, long weekends at other holidays, and variable summer visits, some lasting several weeks at a time. John was married again to Carol, a "nice lady," and the children grew to feel as if they had two homes.

She was their mother! She had given birth to them. She loved them as much as her own flesh, took care of their needs and all of their day-to-day nurturing. Yet here they were in someone else's family picture!

One day, they came home to Fran and showed her a family picture taken at Christmas when they were with their dad. There they sat, nicely posed, with their father behind them, Carol with her child beside her, and on her lap—the new baby.

This nice-looking family group, smiling all around, was like a stab to Fran's heart. She was their mother! She had given birth to them. She loved them as much as her own flesh, took care of their needs and all of their day-to-day nurturing. Yet here they were in someone else's family picture! They had this totally separate life of which she was not a part—and would never be a part. There was the ex-husband, with whom she had given birth to her babies, with another woman and another baby—a token of *their* union—a forging symbol of their new family—a family in which her children had a place but she did not.

80

For a few moments it was very difficult to accept the breadth of meaning in that picture. Those children, which are hers, are also John's, and they truly do have two families and two family lives, and she is not a part of one.

Fran knows that for the children's sake she must not show antagonism, no matter how it hurts. She believes it's better for them to have two lives than one life with her and a "nothing" life with their dad. Many children of divorce living with their mom feel that times with their dad are only visits, little forays into another world, a vacation. She should, Fran tells herself, be happy that her children have a real life with their dad, that he is actively involved with them and not just someone they go visit.

But if he is an active part of their lives, that means they also share in his life—and his new family.

How painful that is for this mother! It means her children have holiday traditions, family idiosyncrasies, even an identity forged apart from the identity they have with her. "Accept it," she tells herself. "Your children have a totally separate life of which you are not a part." She knows it, she says it, but that does not make it easy or hurt any less.

◆

Dear Lord, help me to accept the things I cannot change. Please keep me away from anger and resentment. Help me, with Your supernatural power, to not be jealous of the life my children have apart from me. Thank You that it is a good life for them and not one of harm or danger. Thank You for helping them to be happy, even when they are not with me. I trust them to Your care.
In Jesus' name, amen.

33

When I Fear for My Children

◆

So do not be afraid of them. There is nothing concealed that will not be disclosed, or hidden that will not be made known. . . . Are not two sparrows sold for a penny? Yet not one of them will fall to the ground apart from the will of your Father. And even the very hairs of your head are all numbered. So don't be afraid; you are worth more than many sparrows
(Matthew 10:26, 29–31).

Many mothers or fathers have much more to worry about during their children's visitation with the noncustodial parent than just the fact that they have a separate life. Not all parents are sure their children are safe. How does a parent cope when the home the children must visit, the home of their other birthparent, is so different from their primary residence?

> *How does a parent cope when the home the children must visit, the home of their other birthparent, is so different from the one of their primary residence?*

Many can identify with the following scenario. Paula divorced Dru for a reason. He is neither kind nor reliable. Though he may or may not have been abusive, his way of living is totally alien to the ordered and secure life that her children live with her. How can she turn them over to him every other weekend? Who will comfort them when they are afraid? Who will help them if they feel sick? Dru is not a nurturing parent. Will his wife, a woman who resents their coming because they remind her he had a life before, feed them well or help them if they need help? Will Dru let them call home if they need reassurance?

They live through the first visit, come home, and seem OK. Paula will question them about their well-being and watch them for signs of stress or trauma. Hopefully she will be able to ask them if they had a good visit, and they will feel free to tell her the truth.

But the children too are in a bind. If they say it was good and they had fun, will their mom feel bad? Will that mean they are being disloyal to the woman who sacrifices so much for them? Will she feel jealous? Maybe they should say it was bad. But if they say it was bad, then she will worry about them and possibly try to fix it so they can't go. And they want to go. They feel the need to know this man who is their father, even if he isn't perfect.

Turning your children over to someone else, even for as short a time as a weekend visit, can be nerve wracking. It is especially difficult at the beginning when there are so many unknowns. You do the best you can about ascertaining their safety.

At the time of the divorce, either a visitation agreement was made with the former spouse or the facts were presented to a lawyer, your lawyer brought them to the judge, and the judge made the decision. Now Paula and the kids must live with it, at least for the time being. There is only one thing left to do—trust those children to God.

◆

Dear Lord, I am so afraid when my children are with their other parent. The court says that they must spend time there. It is difficult for them, so uncertain, maybe even scary. Please protect them, Lord—physically, emotionally, and spiritually. In Jesus' name, amen.

34
When Visits Threaten the Well-Being of the Children

◆

In this you greatly rejoice, though now for a little while you may have had to suffer grief in all kinds of trials. These have come so that your faith—of greater worth than gold, which perishes even though refined by fire—may be proved genuine and may result in praise, glory and honor when Jesus Christ is revealed (1 Peter 1:6–7).

I t was one of the worst night-mares of a marriage—the husband was guilty of sexually abusing the children. While Max was serving his jail sentence, the couple were divorced. Max, greatly shamed, sought counseling. His daughters, though scarred, have healed through the love and pa-tience of Terri, their mother, their grandparents, and other family and community members. Their therapy continued even longer than their father's, and at times, both the father and the abused children were counseled together. In the safety of the counseling sessions they were able to see his broken heart and receive his apology. They were able to forgive him. Now the time has come when the children need to spend time with their father. He is married again, and his new wife will be present during their visits. Yes, they may stay overnight at times.

Rather than loosing their faith, this night-marish trial became a way that this mom and her children "proved their faith genuine."

You can imagine Terri's apprehension over her children's safety. You can imagine the children's own fear and reluctance to go. Still, Max is their father. They have loved him and felt loyal to him, even when the abuse was going on. The counselor has helped them to understand him quite a bit. They are as ready as they will ever be—they must go.

Before they leave for the visit, they pray with Terri and fill up with Scripture—verses like "When I am afraid, I will trust in You" (Psalm 56:3) and "The eternal God is your refuge, and underneath are the everlasting arms" (Deuteronomy 33:27a). And for Terri, "Peace I leave with you; my peace I give you" (John 14:27). While the children are gone, Terri and her new husband and some of the stepsiblings pray. So do grandpas and grandmas on all sides.

The children are safe. Their past experience is now a protection, and so is the security of a kind stepmother. They seem to have a good time. They are glad to see their father. Sure, there is forever an ill-at-ease feeling. But they feel a need to be a part of his life. On some visiting dates there are last-minute excuses, not too fervently argued, just "Maybe I'll stay home this time." And Terri must somehow decide what is good and best for the children and encourage them to go, even while she herself is not thrilled about it.

The miracle of this family may very well be that neither Terri nor her children have lost their faith through the evil experience that they endured. Both Terri and her kids say, "Lost our faith? Our faith has seen us through. God was our strength and still is!" Sure, they were angry, plenty of the time, at both God and their father. But God has proven faithful to them in ways that no one can see. And they profess His name and tell of His healing power in their lives.

No, rather than losing their faith, this nightmarish trial became a way that this mom and her children "proved their faith genuine," resulting in praise, glory, and honor to Jesus Christ.

◆

Dear Lord Jesus, evil is very hard, even impossible, to understand. But we know that we live in a world filled with evil, and sometimes it touches us. Thank You that even though it seemed You did not intervene at the time of evil, You have not abandoned us. Thank You that Your heart breaks, as ours does, over the bad that is done. May Your people in many places, faced with various trials, be able to hold fast to their faith and, having proved it genuine, bring all the praise, glory, and honor to You. Amen.

35
Acceptance by Friends

◆

I give you a new commandment that you love one another. Just as I have loved you, you also should love one another. By this everyone will know that you are my disciples, if you have love for one another (John 13:34–35 NRSV).

When Rog and I considered marriage, we realized one of our major questions would be, "Where will we go to church?" For both of us, our involvement in church had always

> I would be moving into his world, but would I fit?

been the major focus of our lives outside the family. For many reasons, I decided that I would join his church and did so before we were married. I knew the final test would be, "How will the people accept me?"

I would be moving into his world, but would I fit? I was not from his ethnic heritage. My gifts are different from his first wife's—would the people compare me to her? They had cared for her needs and ministered to the family so faithfully during her illness. Could they, with all that emotional baggage, receive me? Or would it be too painful for them? You can imagine that I made this a subject of much prayer!

Relief flooded over me the day in church that a dear, white-haired saint, one we all call "Grandma Christians," threw her arms around me after a service and said, "Welcome, dear, you are an answer to our prayers!" Another lady told of watching Rog walk into a service with those three little girls one Sunday and noticed that one wore a sash tied in front that was meant to be tied in back, her sister had on a summer dress in fall, and the third wore sandals on too cool a day.

These are not life-warping or earth-shattering problems by any means! Of course the children were clean, well fed, and loved. But to this day, those three girls and their dad just radiated "we need a mom." So she sat through the entire service praying that God would send them one! And she told me that she was now thanking God that He had sent me.

Another saint came up to me the week after we announced our engagement and told me how wise God was. She said she thought the best thing for Rog would be a woman with no children so the girls wouldn't have to struggle with competition. She had prayed this way. "But," she continued, "God knew better than I did. He sent someone that would understand the grief of Rog's widowhood, who had sons to be brothers but no daughters to compete. What could be more perfect?" So she welcomed me and blessed God that He had a better idea than she did!

And all of them, plus many more, showered me with cards of welcome and well-wishes.

I could continue on and on with stories of how the wonderful people of Hillside Community Church made me welcome in their midst. But I won't. Many readers will identify more with the rejection I've talked about elsewhere. But for now, I want to thank God again and give Him praise, glory, and honor for the way He worked in His people to bring me to a new church home, the one He chose for our blended family.

———————◆———————

Thank You, Lord God of heaven and earth, for hearing our petitions for guidance. Thank You that You were at work, preparing a church where we could be together even before we ourselves knew how to pray. Thank You for the saints that make up Your body, the church, everywhere. Sometimes those who are called Christian do not live up to their calling. But thank You for all the ways and the times that we have lived up to it—the times we have loved one another as Christ has loved us. Thank You for the love You allowed to be poured out on me at a time when I really needed it. In the name of Your Son, who makes all believers one, amen.

36
Rocking Chair Mothers

◆

As a mother comforts her child, so will I comfort you (Isaiah 66:13a).

But the plans of the Lord stand firm forever, the purposes of his heart through all generations (Psalm 33:11).

I will sing of the Lord's great love forever; with my mouth I will make your faithfulness known through all generations (Psalm 89:1).

I n thinking about the people who made me feel welcome when I became a part of Rog's life, I remember a story told by a friend named Donna. She was close to my husband's first wife and a friend he could call for help when the children were sick and the after-school caretakers couldn't fill in the morning gap.

> *The big old rocking chair in the dim living room seemed to call us. There we talked about their day, and gently and gradually I learned about each girl.*

One day before Rog and I were married, little Lisa ran one of those mysterious fevers of early childhood and spent the morning at Donna's house instead of at kindergarten. This volunteer mom's arms were a cradle for Lisa that day, and as Donna rocked the feverish five-year-old, Lisa whispered to her the glad information, "Margaret rocks me too!" At that moment this wonderful family advocate thanked God that I was "the rocking type."

Much later, Donna related this little incident to me and how relieved Lisa's single remark made her feel. Those friends loved my husband's young family, adored the little girls, and very naturally were somewhat apprehensive when he announced that he would marry someone they didn't know.

Donna and the other women in this social group had prayed faithfully for the family, for Rog's finding a wife, and that she (I) would be a good mother to his daughters. Then Lisa told her that "Margaret rocks me too." Donna thanked God that Lisa's stepmom-to-be was the rocking type and in that moment was reassured that God was answering their prayers. For myself, I felt pleased to hear this story and glad that my coming into their lives decreased rather than increased their fears.

"Margaret rocks me too" meant a lot more than I just rocked the

88

children sometimes. When Rog and I were dating and would include the children, I had to find some way to close the day, some nice way to leave. And the big old rocking chair in the dim living room seemed to call us. While the others played in the basement or waited in a bedroom, I would rock one child at a time. There we talked about the day, and gently and gradually I learned about each girl. It was in the rocking chair that Tammy hinted at the pain of her grief, in the rocking chair that Becky could relax and accept affection, and in the rocking chair where Lisa could feel comforted and safe.

Of course my boys had to have a turn too, and so we began what became a family ritual. These children were not babies. At ten, nine, eight, seven, and five, they were probably too big to rock. But that never entered my mind. In all my years as a big sister, child-care giver, and teacher, I had learned the best thing to do for a kid is what your heart tells you they need, not what may seem logical.

Donna's story also made me think of my own mother. She was the "rocking type" too. I can see her still, sitting in the family platform rocker with one of my younger siblings in her lap. And she would rock me, even when I was way too big for such a thing. It was our family place to go for solace and comfort—the safe place for healing talks and soothing fears. In our family you were never too old to get rocked.

My grandma too had been the "rocking type." In holding one of her numerous grandchildren, she beautifully illustrated the generations faithful to showing God's love to their children and grandchildren.

From my family of origin to my nuclear family to my blended family, I brought the tradition of the rocking chair. I guess you could say it was in a rocking chair that we became a blended family. No, we did not instantly and magically all start to love each other. That takes time. I don't want anyone to believe that in one romantic, magical rock of a chair we lived happily ever after. There've been way too much work, frustration, adjustment, and determination involved in our blending for that to be true. But in the rocking chair, affection, understanding and acceptance began, making room for love to grow.

———◆———

Thank You, God, for giving me a mom who rocked me so I could be the "rocking type" of mom. In Your name I pray, amen.

37
A Godly Father

◆

By wisdom a house is built, and through understanding it is established
(Proverbs 24:3).

[Jesus said] I will show you what he is like who comes to me and hears my
words and puts them into practice. He is like a man building a house who
dug down deep and laid the foundation on rock. When a flood came, the
torrent struck that house but could not shake it, because it was well built
(Luke 6:47–48).

This is the victory that has overcome the world, even our faith. Who is it that
overcomes the world? Only he who believes that Jesus is the son of God
(1 John 5:4b–5).

A popular picture in many Christian magazines and in Christian book stores is a print of a father kneeling in prayer by his sleeping child's bed. It is titled simply: "Spiritual Warfare." I love that picture for it reminds me of my own dad. I don't know if he ever came and knelt over me while I slept, but I do know that he prayed for me and brought our family to his Lord every morning of his life. One of my fondest memories is seeing my father sitting at the kitchen table in the wee hours of the morning, reading his Bible and praying. No matter how early he had to get up for work (and the hour changed through the years as the jobs changed), he would always get up earlier in order to have his quiet time with the Lord.

As a child and a young adult, knowing my father began each day with God gave me a great sense of security.

As a child and a young adult, knowing my father began each day with God gave me a great sense of security. No matter how crazy things got in our big family, no matter what our upheaval or struggles, I always knew my dad was praying for me, for us. One time when I was really little, I asked him what he prayed about. He told me his prayers included many things, but always included prayers for his children. Like the father in the painting, my father has gone before the Lord many times, doing spiritual warfare against the forces of evil that challenge his family and his home.

But my father's quiet time did not only include prayer, it also included Bible study. For, as the verse says, a man who "comes to me and hears my words" is like one who builds his life down deep in a solid rock foundation. Parents, we must come to God's Word daily in order to hear the Lord speak to us about our families and our lives.

I pray that every dad who reads this book may understand the importance of spending time with God every day. There really is a battle going on for our children, for all of us. The only way we can win over sin in our lives and in our homes is if we come to God every day, letting Him speak to us and unburdening ourselves to Him. The Word gives guidance for living, and prayer releases the power of God into a situation. Build your foundations deep in the solid rock. Spend time every day in the Word and in prayer.

◆

Dear Father God, thank You for my own Christian father. And please empower dads everywhere to go to battle in prayer for their children. May their children become Your children through the power of Your Word, the power of their fathers' examples, amen.

38
Noncustodial Stepmothers' Dilemma

◆

*Her children arise and call her blessed; her husband also, and he praises her:
"Many women do noble things, but you surpass them all." Charm is deceptive,
and beauty is fleeting; but a woman who fears the LORD is to be praised.
Give her the reward she has earned, and let her works bring her praise at the
city gate (Proverbs 31:28–31).*

Though a stepmother's husband may very well "call her blessed," it is very seldom that she will receive the "reward she has earned" from her stepchildren. As long as there is another mother in the picture, a stepmom will probably be overlooked when it comes to handing out praise.

After talking with so many stepmothers, I want to shout, "Face it, twentieth-century Americans, the stepmothers of this country by-in-large do the parenting when the noncustodial children come to visit!" Even if the father is involved with the kids, she is still the one who probably will cook for them, do their laundry, and may very well chauffeur them, too. If the children come for summer-long visits, she probably buys them clothes and maybe even takes them to the doctor. In other words—she does for them all the same things she does for her own. But she doesn't get the joy of being called "mom" or of being "praised in the city gates" (in public) for being their mother. (After all, in most stories the stepmother is still "wicked"!) On Mother's Day, will the stepchildren remember to honor her? From whom will she ever receive thanks for all she does for them?

Before I get too heavy with the blame here, perhaps I need to think about the children's point of view. For one thing, they didn't ask for this woman in their life. They would probably be happier, or think they would, if their birthparents were together. This just happens to be the woman their father married. Fathers, then, must lead the way in teaching their children to honor both their birthmother and their stepmother. It is by his example that they will learn to send cards and buy thoughtful,

> *The stepmothers by-in-large do the parenting when the non-custodial children come to visit! . . . Fathers, then, must lead the way in teaching their children to honor both their birthmother and their stepmother.*

personal gifts. If their father points out all that their stepmother does, they will see it more readily than if left to notice it on their own. If they see their father showing kindness, thoughtfulness, and gratefulness to his wife and if they can get beyond the jealousy they may feel for the sake of their birthmother, then they MAY give their stepmother the praise and honor that is due her.

Many popular greeting cards now include stepmother cards and "you are like a mother to me" cards. In addition to sending cards, ways to honor stepmoms include time, talk, and understanding—time for the old wounds to heal, talk by both parents about what they expect from the kids when they visit, and hopefully, understanding will be reached by both children and parents about their roles in each other's lives.

In the meantime—stepmothers unite to encourage each other! We are worth honor and praise for our faithful service to our husband's children. Speak up, say how you feel! Act in a way that shows you expect honor and respect, and with your husband's support, you will get it.

◆

Dear God, thank You for all the stepmothers in all kinds of blended families who do "temporarily-on duty" mothering. Work in the lives of their husbands and children to give them the honor and appreciation they deserve. In Your Son's name we pray, amen.

39

What It Means to Fear God

◆

Charm is deceptive, and beauty is fleeting; but a woman who fears the LORD is to be praised (Proverbs 31:30).

It [the church] was strengthened; and encouraged by the Holy Spirit, it grew in numbers, living in the fear of the Lord (Acts 9:31b).

The phrase "a woman who fears the Lord" from Proverbs in devotion 38 echoed in my mind. I asked, "What does it really mean to be a stepparent who fears the Lord, and what does it mean to live in the fear of God?"

Looking in my commentary, I found that in Acts 9:31 the phrase "the fear of the Lord" expresses the holy walk of the early Christians. Holy means belonging to God or set apart for God. So apparently the Christians of the early church lived lives that were set apart for God. They obeyed His commands and lived in a way that caused others to call them "holy."

I apply to myself the payment Christ made to God for me. This is the beginning of living a life "in the fear of the Lord."

Where does this holiness come from? How does a life of "fearing the Lord" begin? There is a beginning for everything, and 2 Corinthians 5:17 talks about beginning a life with Christ: "Therefore, if anyone is in Christ, he [she] is a new creation, the old has gone, the new has come!" How does this new creation start? From where does this new life come? Verse 18, from the *Living Bible* explains, "All these new things are from God who brought us back to himself through what Christ Jesus did."

My sin, the sins I commit willfully and with intention as well as the very basic depravity of my nature, all of my sin, separates me from the Holy God who is perfect in every way. It is this sin and sinful nature of mine that Christ came to do something about. Verse 19 from the same text continues, "For God was in Christ, restoring the world to himself, no longer counting men's sins against them but blotting them out" (TLB). Christ made a way for me to reestablish contact with God, my Creator, by paying the penalty for all my sin and thereby removing the sin barrier that separated me from God.

The question then becomes, Do I believe this, and have I received this for myself? It's one thing to know and believe that I am a person for whom Christ died. It is something else again to say, "I accept this gift of forgiveness for all my sins. I apply to *myself* the payment Christ made to God for me." This is the beginning of my new creation, my new life in Christ, the beginning of living a life "in the fear of the Lord."

If I, a stepparent, am living in the fear of the Lord, if I have become a new creation in Christ, how will this being "reconciled" with God make a difference for me?

The Christians mentioned in the book of Acts were strengthened and encouraged by the Spirit as they walked in the fear of God. We can become strengthened and encouraged for our awesome task of stepparenting when we allow the Spirit of God to fill us to overflowing. We can receive encouragement and love from the Spirit through the Word of God when we walk "in the fear of the Lord."

Remember my friends Rob and Roxie? In a previous devotion I talked about the power of God's Word in their lives and how their whole relationship, even their home, changed as they filled their minds with God's Word. This is one of the ways being reconciled with God can make a difference in one's life.

They had believed in Christ their Savior and been in the church for a couple of years. But when they showed that they walked in the fear of the Lord by reading God's Word, talking about it with each other, and praying together, their intimacy grew, and the stability of their home increased. Previously, there was never enough time for relationships; now they are still busy, but things are more sane and more correctly prioritized as they practice a quiet time together. And the wonderful bonus is this quiet time with God and each other overflows into talking and sharing with their children.

In our own family it's been our time spent "in the fear of the Lord," having family devotions around the table each evening, that's been the primary time of bonding, mending, healing, and sharing—all the things that have made us into a "blended family."

◆

Dear Lord Jesus, thank You for dying for my sins. Thank You that I can live a life guilt-free and connected with God. Thank You for Your Spirit who encourages and teaches me from Your Word, the Bible. Please help me daily to live as one who truly is walking in the fear of the Lord. In Your name, and for Your glory, amen.

40
New Life: Forgiveness

◆

Be kind and compassionate to one another, forgiving each other, just as in Christ God forgave you (Ephesians 4:32).

Bear with each other and forgive whatever grievances you may have against one another. Forgive as the Lord forgave you. And over all these virtues put on love, which binds them all together in perfect unity (Colossians 3:13–14).

For if you forgive men when they sin against you, your heavenly Father will also forgive you. But if you do not forgive men their sins, your Father will not forgive your sins (Matthew 6:14–15).

Probably the greatest thing about being "a new creation in Christ" is becoming a forgiven one. I have a clean slate and can make a new start. I am totally and completely a new person. Everything between God and me is fresh and new, and I am free to begin my new life in Christ. But real life is not just Christ and me. In real life I must learn how being "a forgiven one" changes the way I relate to those around me.

> *If you really are a forgiven one, you will be one who forgives.*

Often the relationships in which I most urgently need a fresh start are the ones where forgiveness is most needed. Once I have acknowledged my own wrongs and failings and know that God has forgiven me, chances are there are also people from whom I need to ask forgiveness.

It is common knowledge that a lot of second marriages fail for the very same reasons the first marriage failed. If you are a divorced person, please, make sure you have identified your part in whatever wrong led to the end of your first marriage. This is the best place to start. Ask forgiveness, then identify the behavior of your ex-spouse that led to the end of your marriage, and tell him or her that you forgive as well. Forgiveness is the beginning of a new life. Having been both forgiven and forgiving, put the past behind and determine through the power of God's Spirit that you will not repeat those mistakes.

In your new marriage, keep short accounts. When you have been hurt, say so, and be quick to forgive. When you have given hurt, admit it, and ask forgiveness. Only by being "new every morning" can your new marriage stay healthy and strong.

If you cannot seem to break out of hurtful patterns, don't give up. Keep a forgiving attitude and get some kind of professional help. You both need to identify what it is that leads you into the negative behavior and how you can break out of those cycles of destruction.

Even though my first marriage did not end because of divorce, there were things for which I felt guilty. Something as simple as, "Why didn't I run out in the morning and kiss him good-bye? He didn't even know I was awake!" gave me pangs of guilt. And there were more serious things, like not saying I was sorry for hurting him. I would think thoughts like, "Oh, I loved him so much. If only I had never said thus and so, or if only I had not done this or that!"

I asked my husband's friend, "What if Bruce didn't even know I loved him? I can't remember when I said it last!" Our friend was sure that my husband knew it; he had no doubts. And as time passed, I believed it too. And I was able to ask God to forgive me even if I couldn't ask my husband. (In my widowed-persons' support group, I learned that this guilt of the survivor is quite commonplace.)

You can be sure that in this marriage I am much quicker to ask forgiveness for specific things when they happen. We have both learned to deal with things when they first arise, before they have had time to simmer and boil over.

The verses above are pretty clear—"If you don't forgive others, God hasn't forgiven you." Bible scholars believe this is not a condition on God's forgiveness but rather the other way around. If you really are a forgiven one, you will be one who forgives. If you don't have the love it takes to forgive, you need to start again with the source—God. From forgiveness we can move to other steps in living a new life. From the power of His Spirit, we can receive the love that is beyond anything we can muster. And with His love we can forgive the most grievous wrong from our past or our present.

◆

Dear Jesus, thank You for dying on the cross to take the penalty for all the things I have done wrong. Thank You for the power of Your Spirit that can enable me to put the past behind and begin anew. Help me to live this day as a forgiven one who forgives others. In Your name, amen.

41
New Life: Bowing Before God

$\blacklozenge$

If you love me, you will obey what I command (John 14:15).

...You shall have no other gods before me. You shall not make for yourself an idol ...You shall not bow down to them or worship them ...
(Exodus 20:1–6).

Jesus replied: "'Love the Lord your God with all your heart and with all your soul and with all your mind.' This is the first and greatest commandment. And the second is like it: 'Love your neighbor as yourself'"
(Matthew 22:37–39).

Another step in living a new life in Christ is growing in obedience to God's Word. The first verse above is bold in its summary of one's deeds. It's simple: If you don't obey God, you don't love God. If your heart is filled with love to Him who gave Himself for you, you will in turn give Him your obedience.

What grabs you so hard around the heart that you are "bowed" before it? To what do you bow other than to God?

Most of you who read this book will be familiar with God's moral law, the Ten Commandments. The first four commandments deal with our relationship with God, and the rest with our relationship with others. When our relationship with God is right, our relationships with others tend to fall into place. The New Testament also has commandments, such as in the third verse above. Let's take a look at the Ten Commandments as they specifically apply to the challenging life of a stepparent, and tie in a New Testament passage that further explains or expands their meaning.

The first commandment reminds us that "You shall have no other god's before me." Do we who call ourselves "Christian" ever have "other gods"? Ask yourself, "What is the most important thing in my life?" Your answer shows what is "god" to you. The way we spend our money, we spend our time, and what we think most about will indicate just what is most important in our lives.

Can we honestly say the most important thing is the God of the Bible? As was discovered by my busy stepparent friends, their relationship to their stepchildren and to each other only improved when God became most important in those relationships. When they found a way to spend time together in His Word and in prayer, other relationships fell into place.

The second commandment reads, "You shall not make for yourself an idol . . . You shall not bow down to them or worship them." What consumes you, stepparent? What grabs you so hard around the heart that you are "bowed" before it? Have you spent so much on clothes, cars, or the house that you are bowed down in debt? Have you been obsessed about your "ex" to the point that you are bowed down with anxiety, hate, or grief? Does your whole life revolve around sports or hunting or golfing or writing or TV or your computer or snowmobiling or any otherwise perfectly good activity to the point that your relationships and your home are burdened down with lack of attention and neglect?

To what do you bow other than to God? Most of the things I mentioned are not wrong. What's wrong is giving them more priority than they should have. They become our idols when the pursuit of pleasure or work is greater than our pursuit of God and the family He has given us to love and serve.

———— ◆ ————

Dear Father God, thank You for Your law that teaches me how to love You and love others. Help me to put You first in my heart and in my life. May I truly have "no other gods" before You. May You be the only One to whom my heart bows. In Jesus' name, amen.

42
Obedient Tongues

♦

You shall not misuse the name of the LORD your God, for the LORD will not
hold anyone guiltless who misuses his name (Exodus 20:7).

With it [the tongue] we bless the Lord and Father, and with it we curse those
who are made in the likeness of God. From the same mouth come blessing
and cursing. My brothers and sisters, this ought not to be so
(James 3:9–10 NRSV).

"Do not let any unwholesome talk come out of your mouths, but only what is
helpful for building others up (Ephesians 4:29a).

When the third command-
ment says, "You shall not
misuse the name of the
LORD your God," it is quite simple
and straight forward—don't take
God's name lightly. This command-

> *"Sticks and stones may break my bones," but words really DO hurt me.*

ment can be a tough one for you to keep, depending on where you work,
how your friends talk, what kind of books you read, and what shows
you watch. But if you are loving God with all your heart, if you intend
to live a life in Christ, the fourth commandment says that you will honor
and respect God's name. If you truly do love God and have misused
His name on occasion, you very well may have felt a pang of grief
and sorrow. Perhaps you have had to ask God for forgiveness.

But besides the dishonor to God, have you ever noticed the broken-
spiritedness of the child or spouse at whom you swear or to whom you
speak hatefully? "Sticks and stones may break my bones," but words
really DO hurt me.

The admonition to not take the name of God in vain is an order for
self-control. Clearly this command, though on the surface dealing only
with your relationship to God, can relate to the way you treat others.

♦

Dear Father in Heaven, help us who call ourselves Your children to obey You.
Thank You that by Your Spirit we are empowered to live in a way that is pleasing
to You and good for us and our family. Thank You that we can "do all things
through Christ who strengthens me" (Philippians 4:13 NKJV) and that all the
things You ask us to do are for our good and for Your glory. In Jesus' name, amen.

43
A Day to Honor God

◆

Remember the Sabbath day by keeping it holy. Six days you shall labor and do all your work, but the seventh day is a Sabbath to the LORD your God. On it you shall not do any work (Exodus 20:8–10a).

The fourth commandment says, "Remember the Sabbath day by keeping it holy." How does your family set aside this special day, a day to honor God? Many Christians throughout history have made lists, much like the Jewish law, of what can and cannot be done on the Lord's

Keeping the Lord's Day special is important to our family, so we do some things to make it special.

Day. "You may only travel so many miles; you must never eat out on Sunday; you must go to church a certain number of times," etc, etc. But rather than setting up "Sabbath rules," we need to "remember the Sabbath," that is, reverence, hallow, keep as special, this day for God.

On Sunday our family worships God in church with other believers. At this time we offer up worship, praise, and honor to Him. We hear sermons that motivate us to live as God would have us live, that build us up to be strong in the kingdom. In addition to our day being for worship, we also spend the day as a family a little differently.

When Rog and I first got married, we noticed how harried and scattered we all became on Sunday when neighborhood children wanted to play all afternoon. We decided to say, "No friends on Sunday. On this day we will worship God together, take our time at dinner, and spend the day with our family."

I do not mean that if you let your kids play with a friend on Sunday you have broken God's law! My intent is to illustrate that keeping the Lord's Day special is important to our family, so we do some things to make it special. Your way of making it special may be different from our way, but God wants His Day to be kept holy. One of the popular catechisms reminds us to limit our activity to "matters of charity and necessity." To me that seems a good guide to follow.

◆

Dear Lord, may we not neglect to set aside a day for You. May we learn on this day to worship and praise You and to rest as You rested. Thank You for the Sabbath day. In Jesus' name, amen.

44

A Command to Honor Our Parents

◆

Honor your father and your mother, so that you may live long in the land the LORD your God is giving you (Exodus 20:12).

"Honor your father and mother"—which is the first commandment with a promise—"that it may go well with you and that you may enjoy long life on the earth" (Ephesians 6:2–3).

Today, as we discuss the fifth commandment, we move away from guidelines for relating to God and on to commandments that teach us how to relate to each other. How we relate to others in the world originates in our homes with our relationship to our parents. God says, "Honor your father and your mother." The dictionary says honor means respect, esteem, pay homage, recognize. Like keeping the Sabbath, your family must find ways to honor your father and mother that work for you and say "honor" to them.*

It's up to us to learn what spells "love" to them.

Many of you who read this book may be part of the "sandwich generation"—you still have dependent children but your parents are also becoming dependent upon you. It can be a very demanding, even draining, time of life. For some, honor may mean making sure that your parents are cared for in a good facility which you visit often, making sure their needs are met and that they are still included in the life of the family through visits, calls, cards, and letters.

Others may have younger parents with whom you have more of an equal, adult friendship, supporting and helping each other the way any committed adults would do. If your parents are far away, calls, sparse visits, and gifts in the mail may be all you can do. The important thing is to give them respect and the recognition that they deserve for raising you. If they have been really lousy parents but you are attempting a relationship, find that one small thing that you remember in a positive light and use it to motivate your heart toward respect and love.

In our blended family we have five grandmothers and two grandfathers. When we were first married, it was seven grandmothers and four grandfathers! Our relationship with each one of them is different; it depends upon their needs, location, and lifestyle. But no matter if we are talking about a grandma in a nursing home or one who is young and independent or one who is preoccupied and busy with her own business or one far away, all of them deserve some honor from us.

What they desire the most is simply to be included in our lives. What this means to the oldest grandmas is regular phone calls and visits. What it means to others is going shopping together, taking care of each other's plants and homes while on vacation, or including them in the children's activities such as school plays and sporting events. What it comes down to is love and respect.

How do we show love and respect to our parents and grandparents? Whatever makes them feel loved and respected! Keep in mind that what may make one person feel loved may do nothing for another. One of our mothers thinks that getting flowers is the absolute most wonderful thing we can do for her. Another grandma really doesn't care for something that lasts so short a time. It's up to us to learn what spells "love" to them.

Know your parents; let them know you. Then you will know what to do for them. Remember, your children are watching, and what they see may very well impact how they treat you when you become the aging parent!

———————◆———————

Dear Lord Jesus, thank You for loving us so that we can love and honor our parents. Thank You for being the perfect Parent to us, so as we begin to parent our parents, we will know how to love them the way that You have loved us. In Jesus' name, amen.

---

*For a devotion on teaching your children to honor their parents, see my book Devotions for the Blended Family (Grand Rapids: Kregel, 1994), #80.

45

Do Not Take Someone Else's Life

◆

You shall not murder (Exodus 20:13).

"I tell you the truth, whoever hears my word and believes him who sent me has eternal life and will not be condemned; he has crossed over from death to life" (John 5:24).

"Death is swallowed up in victory. O death, where is thy sting? O grave, where is thy victory?"... But thanks be to God which giveth us the victory through our Lord Jesus Christ (1 Corinthians 15:54b–55, 57 KJV).

The sixth commandment tells us that God does not want us to take the life of another. You, as readers of this book, are not likely to murder in its usual sense, but the whole issue of euthanasia and aging parents may very well be on the minds of some. Others may struggle over how to deal with the birth of a very premature infant or one that has been born with something very wrong. I cannot discuss in one paragraph what entire books and treatises are being written on today. Just try to keep in mind that there is a huge difference between saving a life and prolonging a death. Try to discern, with the help of the doctors, which of these it is, and don't drag out a death that could be a beautiful home going. I will illustrate from my own experience.

There is a huge difference between saving a life and prolonging a death. . . . It is much easier to know when it's time to go when you know where you are going.

My Smith father-in-law was a doctor practicing medicine full time when he had a heart attack at age seventy-four. At first it was expected that he would make a full recovery, but he never left the hospital. Grandpa Smith had always talked about the absurdity of prolonging death when his greatest joy would be to go to be with his Lord. He was entirely confident that the moment he left his earthly body, he would be in heaven with a wonderful new body. There he would sing praises around the throne of God with his son, brother, and best friend who had all gone before him. And he does so love to sing!

I was there the morning of the day he died. As his breathing became increasingly labored and his color became more and more gray, he said to me, "It looks like I'll be seeing Bruce soon." Having sat beside many deathbeds, he knew his time was coming. As I told him goodbye, my tears were mixed with the comfort of knowing that he would soon be in heaven with the God he loved and the son (my first husband) he missed.

Later that morning, in the indecision of an urgent moment, medical personnel put him on a respirator. Now the family stood around as the nurse demonstrated how the machine was keeping him alive. They couldn't say for sure how long he would live with the machine, but it seemed there was no life without it, and conscious moments were coming further and further apart.

In one lucid moment as he heard what they were discussing, he clearly pointed upward before once again passing out. There was no question to them what he wanted. Soon after, they turned off the machine, and my mother-in-law stood with her family and prayed her husband into eternal life. It was the saddest-gladdest moment in the lives of each one there.

It is much easier to know when it's time to go when you know where you are going. Being forgiven and being sure of heaven and eternal life are the greatest gifts that become ours when we begin our new life in Christ.

───────◆───────

Dear Lord Jesus, thank You for taking the punishment for the sins of all Your children so we can be sure of eternal life. Thank You for the comfort we have when we know our loved one is confident of their eternal destination. But Lord, when we are not sure when it is the right time to "let someone go," please be with us. Give us wisdom. Help us to know what is right and pleasing and obedient to You. In your most holy and precious name we pray, amen.

46
New Life: Obeying God

We know that we have come to know him if we obey his commands. The man who says, "I know him," but does not do what he commands is a liar, and the truth is not in him. But if anyone obeys his word, God's love is truly made complete in him (1 John 2:3–5a).

You shall not commit adultery. You shall not steal. You shall not give false testimony against you neighbor. You shall not covet. (Exodus 20:14–17a).

"You have heard that it was said, 'Do not commit adultery. But I tell you that anyone who looks at a woman lustfully has already committed adultery with her in his heart. If your right eye causes you to sin, gouge it out and throw it away. It is better for you to lose one part of your body than for your whole body to be thrown into hell (Matthew 5:27–29).

Adultery is one of the most common reasons for divorce. Those of you who have been hurt by it will have no problem understanding why adultery is prohibited by God. Whether you or your

> **How can we obey if we don't know how God wants us to live?**

spouse is the one who sinned (or both of you), you know the pain and suffering that was caused by breaking the marriage vow "to leave all others and cleave only to you." Not only does adultery destroy the oneness of marriage, it often spells destruction for the entire family structure. The verses from Matthew above are the words of Christ—a solemn warning to gouge out your eye rather than let your eye lead to sin.

The eighth commandment says, "You shall not steal." A simple four words, yet a command that helps to preserve the social order. If individual property rights are not respected, violence and chaos reign. Just as with adultery, the sin of stealing is preceded by the sin of coveting—the wandering eye, looking on what is not yours and longing for what belongs to someone else.

It is no wonder that in the tenth commandment God says, "You shall not covet your neighbor's house, or wife, or servant, or livestock, or anything that belongs to your neighbor." It is the coveting of those things that leads to the sins of stealing and of adultery.

Then, of course, we must lie to cover up the wrong deeds, and the ninth commandment reminds us that we cannot lie, either about our own deeds or against our neighbor. We lie to ourselves when we say, "I can look, I can covet, as long as I don't touch." We lie when we try to cover up the touching and the taking and when we blame others instead of taking responsibility for ourselves. We lie, trying to hide our sins instead of honestly dealing with our wrongdoings, which leads to repentance and a clean conscience.

If we lie to ourselves and to others about what we have done wrong, we will never become forgiven. If doing wrong is not something you try to avoid; if, when you do sin, it does not grieve you, does not drive you to ask God for forgiveness, then as the first text above says, "You do not know God." For, "If you love me, you will keep my commandments."

Take a look at that sentence again, "If you love me, you will . . ." I love how the Bible says not just, "Don't, don't," but also says, "Do, do." For almost every prohibition in Scripture, an affirmation can be found.

For example, "You shall not commit adultery" (Exodus 20:14), but "husbands ought to love their wives as their own bodies" (Ephesians 5:28). "You shall not give false testimony against your neighbor" (Exodus 20:16), but "love your neighbor as yourself" (Matthew 19:19). "Therefore each of you must put off falsehood and speak truthfully to his neighbor, for we are all members of one body" (Ephesians 4:25). And the classic, "He who has been stealing must steal no longer, but must work, doing something useful with his own hands" (Ephesians 4:28a). The biblical challenge to obey God is a positive challenge, full of encouragement for the right actions—not just prohibition against the wrong.

We have now ever-so-briefly summed up God's moral imperative. After forgiveness, if we are living a new life in Christ, obedience should follow. I want to also emphasize, however, that we obey not because we fear judgment but out of hearts of gratitude for our salvation. In the words of the old hymn, "He gave, He gave, His life for me, what can I give to Him?"

No one, until heaven, will obey God perfectly. In devotions 47–49, I'll discuss why one who really does love God sometimes does sin, and what happens next.

---◆---

Dear God my Creator, thank You that You care so much for me that You give me faithful and good instructions for living. Your Law is good. Help me to have a heart of obedience. Through the power of the Holy Spirit and in the name of Your Son I pray, amen.

47
Some Reasons Why We Sin

◆

I appeal to you therefore, brothers and sisters, by the mercies of God, to present your bodies as a living sacrifice, holy and acceptable to God, which is your spiritual worship. Do not be conformed to this world, but be transformed by the renewing of your minds, so that you may discern what is the will of God—what is good and acceptable and perfect (Romans 12:1–2 NRSV).

I do not understand what I do. For what I want to do I do not do, but what I hate I do . . . For in my inner being I delight in God's law; but I see another law at work in the members of my body, waging war against the law of my mind and making me a prisoner of the law of sin at work within my members. What a wretched man I am! Who will rescue me from this body of death? Thanks be to God—through Jesus Christ our Lord! (Romans 7:15, 22–25a).

No temptation has seized you except what is common to man. And God is faithful; he will not let you be tempted beyond what you can bear. But when you are tempted, he will also provide a way out so that you can stand up under it (1 Corinthians 10:13).

Please read the above Scriptures carefully. They illustrate the ongoing battle in the heart of Paul the apostle. Even when a person has been made new in Christ, the battle continues between the new nature and sin. The world is all around us with its temptations and anti-God logic. We sin because we allow our minds and hearts to be filled up with messages of the world that oppose what God has to say.

Sonja had a weak marriage and indulged her desire for romance by filling her mind with soap operas and racy novels. The plots of these stories continually justify giving in to passion, explain away "falling in love" with someone other than a spouse because "I just can't help it," and include the voyeurism of bedroom scenes that are more exciting and fulfilling than anyone's

> *Even when a person has been made new in Christ, the battle continues between the new nature and sin. . . . We allow our minds and hearts to be filled up with messages of the world that oppose what God has to say.*

reality. Sonja's discontent mounted, and by the time an interested fellow came into her life, this ordinary woman had become weak and willing to succumb. Rather than change her desire, she fed it with destructive messages she did not choose to edit from her mind and heart. For the passion of a love affair, she left her husband and children.

We may identify with Sonja as we see seeds of our own problems blooming in her. But if we look closely enough, we acknowledge that she fed her miseries with what she put into her mind. The choice to end her marriage was really made over many years as she spent more time thinking about (coveting) what she didn't have than over rejoicing in what she had. Often, as is mentioned in the first Scripture above, our passionate sins spring from a heart filled with wrong desires.

The third verse above talks about God being faithful to provide a "way to escape" temptation. The way to prevent sin is to start at the origin, at the heart, and replace wrong thinking with right thinking. Psalm 119:11 says, "I have hidden your word in my heart that I might not sin against you." Oh that Sonja would have done that!* Hiding God's Word in our hearts is the strongest deterrent to sin.

————◆————

Dear Lord Jesus, please help me to desire obedience; help me edit what goes into my mind and heart. Help me to fill up on the truth and power of Your Word, and give me the desire to guard myself against the enticements and lies of the world around me. Amen.

———

*I know it takes two to make a marriage work or fail. But for the sake of illustration, I chose to discuss only her side.

48
Strength and Encouragement for Obedience

◆

No temptation has seized you except what is common to man. And God is faithful; he will not let you be tempted beyond what you can bear. But when you are tempted, he will also provide a way out so that you can stand up under it (1 Corinthians 10:13).

When tempted, no one should say, "God is tempting me." For God cannot be tempted by evil, nor does he tempt anyone; but each one is tempted when, by his own evil desire, he is dragged away and enticed. Then, after desire has conceived, it gives birth to sin . . . (James 1:13–15a).

As we discussed yesterday, filling our minds with wrong messages is one of the reasons we sin. Where we put ourselves is another reason. Do we hang around what tempts us and "hope for the best" while really desiring the worst? For example, if you feel tempted to overspend and covet material possessions—stay out of the mall! Don't watch the shopping channel!

Do you need to put yourself in a different place, run for help, or renew your mind with different messages? If you search your heart, you will know how to keep from sin.

Remember the story of Joseph in the Old Testament? He fled from the seductive wife of Potiphar rather than allow himself to succumb to her wiles. Although it would be some years before he saw it, Joseph's life was immensely blessed by God because of his obedience. (His story can be found in the book of Genesis. Chapter 39 deals with this temptation.) Where he put himself was his key to obedience.

Kate was very tempted to commit adultery. She was well aware of the fact that it was pure lust. She actually convinced herself she could commit adultery and no one would get hurt, no one would find out. But because of her marriage vows and her commitment to God, she "ran."

She couldn't run away from her job, but she "ran" to a friend. Kate made herself accountable to Judy, a mature Christian woman. Judy understood Kate's desires but also prayed with her and encouraged her to obey God. When Kate's accountability to God was weak, she became accountable to Judy. Judy called Kate every few days and prayed with her.

Within one week of seeking her accountability partner, the nature of the relationship Kate had with the man changed completely, and the temptation was gone. She was able to finish her weeks in association with this man without any further desire for him. Kate "ran" to an accountability partner (who held her accountable to God), and it saved her! It was the position in which Kate put herself that determined whether or not she gave in to temptation.

My own temptations to sin are usually against my family. I want to yell at people, say any number of unkind things, and just generally let them "have it." My husband assures me that I can be very cruel with my tongue at times. These situations usually occur when I am tired and/ or pressured. Sometimes I am sick of kids and worn out.

But before you say, "Poor her, I know how she feels," let's take a look at how I got so tired and pressured in the first place. Did I stay up too late reading? Did I set up too many summer visits from too many people? Did I say "yes" to too many projects or talk on the phone too long to someone? Is there not enough time to get supper on or enough of "me" for the family when I turn from what I've been doing to their demands and needs?

Take a look at your own sin patterns. What triggers sin for you? The old Calvinists used to call them "besetting sins." What are the ones that seem to "get you" every time? Can you see where you could have prevented it if you had gotten your heart and mind under control a few steps back? Do you need to put yourself in a different place, run for help, or renew your mind with different messages? If you search your heart, you will know how to keep from sin.

And finally, when I am up against it, when all the prevention has still led to the breaking point, when I am so tired and irritable that I can almost feel an explosion before it happens, do I call on God to strengthen and help me stay in control? He promises that when we are tempted to blow it, He will provide "a way to escape."

———————◆———————

Thank You, Lord, that You have promised always to provide a way to escape our sin. Thank You for never asking us to do anything without providing the power to obey. Amen.

49
When We Fail

◆

Jesus answered, "A person who has had a bath needs only to wash his feet; his whole body is clean. And you are clean ..." (John 13:10).

If we confess our sins, he is faithful and just and will forgive us our sins and purify us from all unrighteousness (1 John 1:9).

So, brothers [and sisters], you have no obligations whatever to your old sinful nature to do what it begs you to do (Romans 8:12 TLB).

No, in all these things we are more than conquerors through him who loved us (Romans 8:37).

It seems we have come full-circle in logic. In devotion 39, I wrote about becoming a new creation in Christ, how one can become forgiven and start a new life. Then I discussed obedience, temptation, sin, and now, the second verse above is again on forgiveness. "But," you may protest, "I am a forgiven one! Why would I ever have to ask forgiveness again?"

> *We are not in perfect communion with Him and need again to receive forgiveness for what we know we should not have done.*

Jesus explained this need to the disciples as He washed their feet in preparation for the Last Supper. At first protesting, but then allowing Jesus to wash his feet, Peter asked the Lord to wash *all* of him (John 13:1–17). But Jesus reminded Peter that he was already a washed one; he had already had a bath. But the part of him that walked in the world, his feet, needed to be cleansed repeatedly.

If we are truly God's children, we have a heart bent toward obeying God. But as illustrated in the past couple of devotions, there is a battle that goes on within us, and sometimes we dirty our feet with sin. Then, although God has not removed His presence from us (Romans 8:38), we are not in perfect communion with Him and need again to receive forgiveness for what we know we should not have done.

I've heard sin compared to a break in the telephone line. We are connected to the phone service, the lines are in, all is in working order. But we can't continue our communication with God if we hang up on Him. He is always "on line," but if we want perfect fellowship (companionship and communication), we need to have no sin between, for sin interferes with our connection.

First John 1:9 is one of the most reassuring verses in the Bible because it reminds us that if we confess, that is, agree with God that we have done wrong, He will forgive us. And He doesn't stop there. If we stay in this mode of agreeing with Him, a confessing state you may call it, He will work away at us, "cleansing us from all unrighteousness."

I wanted to end this whole section on obedience, sin, and temptation on the most encouraging and positive note possible, so I chose the Romans texts above. We don't HAVE to sin. We are not, the first verse assures, obligated to sin; we are new—period. And as the last verse says, we are MORE than conquerors!

My tempted but victorious friend (from devotion 48) rejoices in her victory. Because of the nature of her story, she can't go around telling it to people, but she wants others to know that the temptation was very real and very strong. On some days, when she was around the man of her desire, she felt powerless. She wanted him.

As I said, she convinced herself that she could get away with the adultery and no one would ever know. Because she does live in this world, she knows how many people view sexual desire—that it is some kind of all-powerful drive that cannot be helped. Listening to these voices, she felt like she almost had to do it, that it was stronger than she was. But when she found a friend to confide in, one who would stand with her in prayer and check on her, the darkness was pierced with the light of truth, and she could again hear God's voice encouraging, "No, in ALL these things we are more than conquerors through him who loves us" (Romans 8:37).

Amen and amen!

———————◆———————

Dear Lord Jesus, thank You that I can do all things through You, the Giver of my strength. Thank You that Your Spirit within me is stronger than any temptation. Thank You that I am MORE than a conqueror because You love me. In Your great name, amen.

50
No Looking Back

◆

Jesus replied, "No one who puts his hand to the plow and looks back is fit for the kingdom of God" (Luke 9:62).

I can do everything through him who gives me strength (Philippians 4:13).

Sometimes, maybe lots of times, stepparenting is just too much. You have all those kids with their needs and demands that seem to never stop. If the children only come sometimes, the family that lives in the house full-time is constantly unsettled by the visits of the children who live there part-time. The work is never done, and the idea of having a loving relationship with this new spouse is a joke. Who has time for a relationship? Both of you must work to make ends meet.

> *Sometimes we may long, if only momentarily, for the simple life we had before. We may think that despite the loneliness of single-parenting, at least life was simpler.*

After work, there are all the ball games. You want to be there for your kid, if not every time, then almost. And going to a game is a good way to show support for that stepchild toward whom you still have ambivalent feelings. Doing it all is not humanly possible! How can you fit everything into this one life that you have been given to live?

Sometimes we may long, if only momentarily, for the simple life we had before. We may think that despite the loneliness of single-parenting, at least life was simpler, "fewer people demanded sections of my life!" Or, you may long for the more distant time—the first marriage. If not longing for the marriage, you may at least long for the life—one set of kids, one spouse, no "ex" in the picture.

But the truth is, though it may have seemed easier back then, things are never going to be that way again. "Going back" is not an option. Perhaps your life was so miserable you never look back and long for the simpler times. But many do. And to those I say, "Hang on! Get thinking straight. Fill up your mind with God's Word."

"Oh great! One more thing to do. When do I have time to read the Bible?" But the point is—the busier you are, the more you need to spend time with God. You can't go back to a simpler life, but each day you can get encouragement, advice, healing, and comfort from God's

Word. Those few moments of meditation in the morning or before bed can revive your spirit, restore your soul, get you thinking "right" and looking optimistically at your present life rather than longing for the past.

So don't look back. Instead look at now. But look through the lens of the Word of God. There is the moral law, the Ten Commandments, that explains of how to relate to both God and man that helps us clearly see right from wrong. In these frenetic days we really need to touch base with the basics, the unchanging, the immutable law of God. Then there are the Proverbs, full of wisdom and advice for living. The stories of Jesus and the letters of the apostles give us a lot of ideas about personal holiness and how to relate to people, especially within the church. These are all reasons that we need to spend a quiet time with God, even if it is only moments a day.

I experienced this need in a most practical way. I grew up knowing the importance of devotions and began having my own quiet time with God when I was still a kid. Of course there were times when I was not so consistent—a devotional book didn't work out so I lost interest or I felt guilty for something and avoided God or I skipped devotions simply because I allowed life to interfere.

But never had I missed so many quiet times as when I became a stepmother! I may have needed it more, but my life became one of constant running from morning to night, and I definitely was spending less time with God. After many weeks I realized it had been a long time since I had taken in God's Word or talked to Him other than at our family devotions. It was also at this time that I experienced the problems with my oldest stepdaughter and wished for the simpler life, the life of a nuclear family with children I was familiar with from birth!

I asked the women's prayer group at church to pray that I would have wisdom. Even as I made my request to them, I recalled a verse from Proverbs: "The fear of the LORD is the beginning of wisdom" (9:10). As that verse came to my mind, I had a sudden flash of insight— in just a couple of minutes a day I could read a proverb. So I began to read a proverb a day.

I couldn't believe it! In two weeks time I told one of the women in the group that I could feel their prayers and that God was telling me what to do with the children a little at a time, one proverb a day. Each day the proverb seemed just what I needed for guidance right then. I relearned what I had learned already so many times in my life—there is wisdom for living in the pages of God's Word and there is power in prayer. Do it! Don't try to live without the Word and prayer.

Instead of looking back and longing for a simpler life, look to the present—but look at it through God's Word. Tap into the power of insight and wisdom on those pages.

◆

Dear Father God, thank You for the wonders of Your Word. Help us, through its pages, to look with wisdom and understanding on the life we live. Please keep us, Lord, focused on You and give us a rational view of the life we live.
In Jesus' name, amen.

51
Time for All Your Children

◆

But I trust in you, O LORD; I say, "You are my God." My times are in your hands" (Psalm 31:14—15a).

He will be the sure foundation for your times, a rich store of salvation and wisdom and knowledge; the fear of the LORD is the key to this treasure (Isaiah 33:6).

Sometimes a child's resentment of the stepparent and step-siblings can be traced to the fact that he or she feels these new people on the scene are taking their birthparent away. It is true that there is only just so much time in the day and strength in a person's body. If a father marries a new wife and takes on her children, it only stands to reason that there will be less time for his birthchildren. Also, if the birthchildren don't live with their dad, there is not only time-competition when they come to visit, they may feel that their dad has deserted them to form a new family and doesn't have an interest in them anymore.

A little creative thinking can give a mom and dad some wonderful ways to spend time with his or her own kids.

Our social worker told us that the single biggest complaint she gets from the children she counsels is that they don't get enough time with their birthparent. Here we were in the beginning days of our marriage, doing everything we could to blend, to be one family, and she was suggesting that we "unblend" and spend time alone with our birthchildren!

It was true. I was spending a lot time with the girls, caught up in fixing hair and selecting clothes. So I decided to make a point of tucking each child into bed every night. I had never missed a night when I had only two, but now I missed often. With five kids, tucking in took a long time, usually an hour or more. But I decided to be faithful to this individual time and it was worth it!

During tucking-in time, we talked about their day, did some reading, sometimes prayed, and sometimes sang—whatever seemed needed. I did this faithfully through elementary school and into junior high. Gradually, as they grew older, I did it less and less. But individual time at the closing of the day helped each child feel that they had had special attention.

Rog could not "get into" tucking them in, after all, that was "my

117

thing." So he began to take a kid along to the hardware store. Each Saturday, he chose a different kid to go to early morning breakfast with him and his brothers. And gradually he got one child or another to help him with Saturday jobs. Also, the kids think is really great when I'm gone in the evening and Rog takes them for ice-cream or they go buy the makings for floats. My absence becomes a special event with dad!

Gradually our lives change, their ages change, and the activities change. But the point is, a little creative thinking can give a dad or mom some wonderful ways to spend time with his or her own kids. Sometimes these ideas will just naturally lead into time with the stepchildren too.

If we stop to think about it, we'd say, "I don't have time!" But if we hold the children as a priority in our lives and bring the time problem to God, the One who is the foundation of our lives, He will take the time of our lives and give us the moments we need to make all our children feel loved and secure. The most important things in both blending with stepchildren and remaining bonded to birthchildren are genuine interest taken and time invested.

———————◆———————

Dear Lord, thank You for being the sure foundation of our times. Thank You for making our time "grow" and giving us the time we need to pay attention to our kids. We can never see how we have enough time, but with our times in Your hands, we have enough after all. Thank You for being our God, Ruler of our lives. In Your glorious name, amen.

52

Stepdad's Balancing Act: Finding Enough Time

by Roger L. Broersma

◆

But seek first his kingdom and his righteousness, and all these things will be given to you as well. Therefore do not worry about tomorrow, for tomorrow will worry about itself. Each day has enough trouble of its own (Matthew 6:33–34).

T he greatest stressor for us step-dads is the balancing act we must do—the challenge of spending enough time with the wife, the children, the job, the church, and still have personal time. I constantly have to deal with the conflict of trying to bond with the stepchildren

> *The world kept screaming that "self" was the most important and that to be healthy, I must put my own needs first.*

while not neglecting my birthchildren or being guilty of doing the reverse.

Of course the demands of a high-pressure job, which often require fifty-five or more hours per week, don't help any. Sometimes, at first, I thought of switching to a less-demanding job with fewer hours, but then again, we need this job to support the family, which grew suddenly from four to seven people!

At various times I have been involved with church activities and offices which I felt were important to God and also needful as an example to my children. All of these things, plus the priority of carving out time for my wife at least once a week, left me feeling, at the beginning of our marriage, that I would never have any time to do the things that I wanted to do.

The world kept screaming that "self" was the most important and that to be healthy, I must put my own needs first. All of these pressures overwhelmed me sometimes, leaving me feeling very inadequate. I could not even begin to meet the ideal image promoted in my Christian community.

As time went on, and with some input from a good Christian counselor, I learned that these demands need not be in conflict with each other at all. And in fact, I didn't have to look at these needs as demands at all but as something good and wonderful. I had to learn to rely on the Lord to give me the strength and wisdom to do the best job that I am capable of doing. God promises that my best will be enough.

I have learned to put Him first, my wife and family next, and quit worrying about "doing my own thing." When my priorities are straight, the guilt is gone, and it is amazing how often I end up doing exactly what I feel I need to do! Time to work on our cars, care for our yard, and work in my workshop really does appear. The worst part was worrying about it all the time—and feeling guilty. But when I put God and my wife and family first, the guilt is gone, and I really do end up having time for the "regenerating" things that bring me peace and a sense of wholeness as a person.

◆

Dear Father God, help fathers, especially fathers of blended families, to know how to put You first. Give us wisdom and sensitivity as we attempt to be all the things that we need to be. In Jesus' name, amen.

53
Tips to Reduce Stepsibling Rivalry

◆

The child grew and was weaned, and on the day Isaac was weaned Abraham held a great feast. But Sarah saw that the son whom Hagar the Egyptian had borne to Abraham [her stepson] was mocking [her son], and she said to Abraham, "Get rid of that slave woman and her son, for that slave woman's son will never share in the inheritance with my son Isaac"
(Genesis 21:8–10).

Stepmoms today are not usually required to live in the same household as the "other wife" with the "other children" as Sarah was! But even so, stepsibling rivalry is one of the fiercest rivalries on earth. Sibling relationships in stepfamilies can vary a lot from family to family. For example, families where the stepsiblings all live together in one house (such as is our case) are quite different from families with a group of kids who live

They came to see you, not your spouse or your stepchildren. . . . Allow the children who live with you to continue their lives with as little interruption as possible when the visiting stepsiblings arrive.

there most of the time and another group of kids who only come for visits.

Since the visits of stepsiblings can cause much disruption in a household's routines, the Stepfamily Association of America* gives some tips for the family that has "visiting children."

First of all, recommends this group of counselors and stepparents, don't force the stepsiblings to do things together. The children have come to spend time with their parent, not with the other kids. It may be that you all would like to do something together, such as a family vacation or an outing. There is certainly nothing wrong with such activities. But don't expect the children to act like you are "all one big happy family," because in their minds you may not be! And when you are not involved in a family activity, certainly don't expect the children you live with to entertain the visiting kids. Again, remember that they came to see you, not your spouse or your stepchildren.

Secondly, maintain a sense of privacy for each child. The visiting child should respect the belongings and space of the child who lives there and vice versa. And when the children do get into inevitable conflicts, parents should not take on those conflicts as their own. Encourage the children to solve their own problems as much as possible; only get involved when you must. Setting limits right away and enforcing property rights can help minimize the rivalry.

I especially liked the final point made in the "tips list" for visiting children. "Don't treat the visiting children as guests. They should be expected to adhere to all family rules and even perform regular chores while they are with you." One of the biggest complaints I've heard from stepparents is that their whole lives are disrupted every time the spouse's children come to visit. Don't let this happen! Allow the children who live with you to continue their lives with as little interruption as possible when the visiting stepsiblings arrive. Keep the family rules the same for all children. If they cause more work by their presence, then they can do chores to help compensate. Working together as well as playing together helps make a family.

◆

Dear Father God, You know how we are made and You know all our flaws and weaknesses as human beings. You understand when our children and stepchildren are jealous of one another. Please give us abundant supplies of wisdom and tremendous amounts of love for all of our children so that the rivalry can be kept to a minimum. Thank You for hearing our prayers. In Jesus' name, amen.

*Stepfamily Association of America, 215 Centennial Mall South, Suite 212, Lincoln, NE 68502 (1-800-735-0329).

54
My Grandma

◆

I have been reminded of your sincere faith, which first lived in your grandmother Lois and in your mother Eunice (2 Timothy 1:5a).

Even when I am old and gray, do not forsake me, O God, till I declare your power to the next generation, your might to all who are to come (Psalm 71:18).

May 1, 1995. Last night my grandma died. She was ninety-one years old and hadn't known who I was for quite awhile. She died with her family around her, holding her hands, telling her they loved her, and saying, "It's OK to go now, to go to God, to go see Grandpa. It's OK to leave. We love you; you're the best grandma!"

> *She died with her family around her, holding her hands, telling her they loved her. . . . She opened her worn black Bible every day to feed her mind and revive her spirit. . . . "She wasn't perfect, you know!"*

I weep for the loss of her, even though I know that it is far better for her now. I really lost her about a year and a half ago when I went to see her and she didn't know me or understand our conversation at all. She didn't even say to the women around her, "This is my granddaughter, she's named after me!" She always used to say that. I wept the most bitter tears that day.

I recalled what she had been to me: a soft arm to lean against in church, a big purse with mints (that were really Tums) and the most interesting coin purse which could hide a penny from a searching little finger for almost a whole sermon! She was a maker of great pies and her famous "blueberry dessert," a seamstress, a crafter, and most of all, a woman of the Word.

She had been a Sunday school teacher for over twenty years, and she had been *my* teacher. She explained to me about mockingbirds, the ways of squirrels in the attic, why the pear tree wasn't good anymore, and how Jesus died to take away my sins. She told lots and lots of stories about when she was young and first married. Most of her stories showed how faith and love get people through the tough times.

Even when her sister died in her arms and a few weeks later her sister's infant child was taken away from her care, even when her own newborn baby died, even then, and in all these things, there is God. She opened her worn, black Bible every day, maybe more than once a day, to feed her mind and revive her spirit. The first time I visited her in the nursing home, she was still doing this, albeit a little confusedly. But the last time I saw her, she couldn't even focus on a pretty quilt well enough to pick it up, let alone read the Bible.

The day I got mad at God and demanded, "What wrong has she ever done? Why did You let her get like this?" my wise, younger sister Bess replied, "Well, Marg, she wasn't perfect, you know!" And we laughed.

Then my sisters and I shared more realistically about grandma. We loved our grandma. She was all the things I said she was in the paragraphs above. But she had her flaws. She could be jealous of the time we spent with our other grandma. She could be short tempered with Grandpa, especially in the afternoon when her blood sugar was low. (But the way she said "your grandpa" was so tinged with love and accompanied by such a twinkle in her eye, we never doubted their love, no matter how grouchy she got. They both had that kind of contended-grin expression that you see on the face of people in a fulfilling marriage.) She liked to hide candies to snack on, and she would share them with us as she whispered, "Don't tell." She collected pretty dishes, saved everything, and filled up every nook and cranny of her house with knickknacks, collectibles, and—junk. So OK, she wasn't perfect! But she was our grandma, we loved her, and it was hard to understand why she had to leave her senses before she left her body.

But that day, as we sisters remembered her together, we realized again how much we learned from her. We learned about family loyalty—and we learned that loyalty includes the families on both sides of our marriages! We learned much about nature and its wonders, and we desired to pass this wonder on to our kids. We learned to praise the Creator. We learned to fill up on the Word and, hopefully, to do it every day in order to "overflow" with it. We learned how God's power gets us through the tough times. And we learned to love our husbands. (I hope that others can see how much I love my husband, just like we all could see how much Grandma loved Grandpa, even though I can get grouchy with my husband too!)

God made Grandma "a beacon to declare God's power to the next generation." We've all been guided by her beacon of faith. My grandma: Margaret Straw-Jordon, 1904-1995.

◆

Dear Jesus, thank You for grandmas and grandpas. Thank You for all that we can learn from them, both the good to embrace and the bad to avoid. Thank You that my life has always been surrounded by the prayers of godly grandparents, and may I be as faithful to the Word and prayer as they. In Jesus' name, amen.

55

Grandpa Timmer: Saint of God

♦

All Scripture is God-breathed and is useful for teaching, rebuking, correcting and training in righteousness, so that the man of God may be thoroughly equipped for every good work (2 Timothy 3:16–17).

Be ye doers of the word, and not hearers only (James 1:22a KJV).

On Memorial Day, May 30, 1881, a boy named John Timmer was born—my daughters' great-grandfather. When little John was only five years old, his mother died. A couple of years later, his father remarried. I don't know if this was a happy blended-home or not, but tragedy struck again for young John Timmer when his father also died just five years later. For a while, he and his sister lived with their stepmother, but soon she too remarried.

It was then that the most awful thing happened. In the days before the welfare system, in the time before licensed foster care homes, this twelve-year-old boy was turned out into the world to fend for himself. The new husband of his stepmother said he would not live in the same house with another man's son, not even for one day. And so, on the very day that his stepmother remarried, he was told to leave. His sister was allowed to stay only until an aunt took her in, and she grew up with that aunt in Grand Rapids, seldom able to see her brother.

The day he was turned out, John had to walk fourteen miles to the home of his stepmother's sister, who let him come and work her farm for his room and board. No more would he have a real family, only a series of places to work and to board. What a terribly lonely and painful time that must have been for the young teen. Many young men, faced with such rejection, would become hardened and bitter. But God had His hand on John Timmer, and even at that awful time, God was at work, molding young John into a man of His design.

> *Many young men, faced with such rejection, would become hardened and bitter. But God had His hand on John Timmer, and even at that awful time, God was at work, molding young John into His design. . . . His children saw him read his Bible every day and live by its teachings.*

John remained in the farming areas of west-central Michigan, going from farm to farm working for anyone who offered him board and perhaps a small wage in exchange for his labor. In the winter he managed to go to school a little, but only made it through grade six. Regardless of his little education, however, he always went to church and read his Bible as his parents had taught him.

When he was about sixteen, he was boarding with a widow lady and her daughter. It seemed that it was an especially trying situation as she barely paid him enough to survive. One day as he labored in the fields, he was overcome with a longing for God. Perhaps it was God's love that he felt in that lonely field. Perhaps he felt anger and wanted to be released from it. Whatever the reason, he dropped his hoe, left the field, and made his way directly to the local church where he told the pastor he wanted to profess his faith in Christ immediately.

What later happened to this highly esteemed man, who came to be called "Grandpa Timmer" by all who knew him, is a story of true blessing. He grew up and was able to buy his own farm. He married and had children. When the children were still young, sadly, his wife died. He vowed never to remarry until the children were grown, not wanting to risk what a stepmother might do to the children he loved. But when they were all grown up, he did remarry, a widow with two children, and so ended up with seven loving children.

And this man was truly loved. Not only did his family find him affectionate, loving, and kind, but many people in his church and surrounding areas felt the touch of his kindness. Always an elder, he ministered to many but took a special interest in the young people, especially the young men, and encouraged them to read their Bibles. If they were a bit rebellious or slow to commit themselves to the Lord, he wrote to them or visited them in person. His love drew many into God's family.

His love for his sister remained in his heart always. When she married, she and her family would come to his farm for two weeks every summer and spend time basking in one another's company and companionship.

But the central focus of his life was God's Word. Not only did he always teach a Bible class to young men, impressing upon them the importance of the Bible in their lives, but he also became a part of the World Home Bible League. As a League representative, he went from home to home each year, collecting money to spread the Word of God around the world. From the story of his own life, he was able to convince many that God's Word makes all the difference.

Because he held the Bible as his highest treasure, whenever a couple in the family would marry, he gave them the greatest gift he could: Scripture verses drawn in colorful designs by his own hand and then framed.

His daughter, Mildred DeKock, my daughters' grandmother on their birthmother's side, calls her father an "always happy, practical Christian, full of joy and love." She says that he taught her and her siblings to hide God's Word in their hearts and to live by its precepts. If he noticed them straying a bit, he would speak to them honestly, openly, and with great love. He always was direct, not shying from sensitive subjects, but applying everything to the Word of God.

If there is anything we can learn from John Timmer's long and faithful life (he lived to be 101!), it is the importance of God's Word and putting God first. His children saw him read his Bible every day and live by its teachings. I challenge every dad who reads this story to do as Grandpa Timmer did: Fill up on God's Word daily and faithfully teach it to your children.

◆

Dear Lord, thank You for Grandpa Timmer and the many lives he touched for the good. May we esteem Your Holy Word as highly as he did, and may we hide it in our hearts. In the name of Your own dear Son, amen.

56
Positive Thoughts—Positive Feelings

♦

Let the peace of Christ rule in your hearts, since as members of one body you were called to peace. And be thankful. Let the word of Christ dwell in you richly as you teach and admonish one another with all wisdom, and as you sing psalms, hymns and spiritual songs with gratitude in your hearts to God (Colossians 3:15–16).

T he verse above is talking about "the body" of the church. But I would like to expand this a little and apply it to being one as a blended family.

When your thinking changes, your emotions and then your actions change.

For example, a stepmom, with a suddenly multiplied number of children, may feel overburdened with caring for all of them. When children come gradually, one at a time, adjustments are difficult; but when kids increase by multiples, adjusting is even more challenging.

When Dorothy first thought of marriage, she saw a man who was like her, a single parent. Bud appeared to do everything for his kids and do it well. Naturally, Dorothy thought he would continue to do it when they got married. But now, here she is for the umpteenth time, stuck in the laundry room for almost an entire day with no help in sight. Dorothy is always yelling at Bud's kids to pick up, and she doesn't feel like he's helping at all.

Dorothy can become filled with anger and resentment, or she can concentrate on filling her mind and heart with the peace of Christ. By practicing being thankful, she may change her resentment into gratitude—thankful that she gets to be the mom of all these kids. By focusing on what God has given her and what He has done and is doing for them (that he made them a family and is giving strength for each day), she can replace her resentment with peace. And a peaceful attitude can help her have a calm approach when she talks things over with her husband and explains the kind of help and support she needs. This will accomplish much more than a yelling tirade!

Then there are the children, who most likely never asked to become stepsiblings. They are forced to share their home, maybe their room and their bathroom space, with these other kids they may not even like. Even if they did like each other to start with, feelings of being invaded and indignation over sharing not only space but parental attention can lead to a real hate-hate relationship. Of course if possible, parents try to give each child time and space. We know the parents of a blended family who finished off the basement of their home into seven separate bedrooms so each child could have their own room, their own private space. But many families cannot do this.

Still, a way needs to be found for the children to be able to view their blending as a blessing—a different way for them to think. If they can comprehend how much better it is for all of them to live in a two-parent home, if they have a relationship with God so they can talk to Him about their situation, if they can learn to be thankful, perhaps they can also learn to live in peace. If they, as well as their parent and stepparent, can learn to turn to the pages of Scripture for instruction on how to live together and how to learn to love, they may learn to have peace in their home.

Bud, who thought he really wanted to be the dad to "all these kids," finds that some of them resent his authority and take offense at his interest in their lives. He wants to be a dad to them, but his idea and their idea about what this means is not the same. And on top of that, they always get into his stuff and leave his tools out in the yard and make a mess in the space that was formerly his. How can Bud and these kids possibly learn to live in peace? How can he think about it all in a more positive way?

If they can find some common ground, some things of mutual interest to do (even if they are parent manufactured—not previous interests), some way to spend positive time together, then they will have some good things to think about.

Changing the focus to what there is to be thankful for in their being together, to what they can agree upon, perhaps will bring them to a peaceful relationship. If they can't seem to "feel" thankful, they probably need to change their thinking. And a good way to do that is to fill up their minds with God's Word.

Our mindsets can be greatly altered, as the verse above says, by letting the Word of God dwell richly in our hearts. Do you need to know how to think? Is anger, resentment, and a sense of being overwhelmed all you can feel? Try filling up your mind with the messages of God's Word. (See devotion 15 entitled "On Being 'The Other' Mom" for some encouraging verses.) When your thinking changes, your emotions and then your actions change.

◆

Dear Heavenly Father, thank You that we don't have to live bogged down in misery and discontent. Thank You that You have given us power to change our despair to hope and our resentment to thankfulness by feasting on Your Word. Thank You for Your Spirit that lives within and empowers us to do all things. Amen.

57

Teens, Teens, Teens!

◆

My child, do not forget my teaching, but let your heart keep my commandments (Proverbs 3:1 NRSV).

Then you will understand what is right and just and fair—every good path. . . . Discretion will protect you, and understanding will guard you. Wisdom will save you from the ways of wicked men (Proverbs 2:9,11–12a).

We have five children, almost all the same age. At the time I write this devotion, they are 13, 15, 15, 17, and 18. Our house has hormones! And oh, the joys they bring! One night we had to deal with three teenage crises all at one time!

Our house has hormones!

Child number one has totally had it with her job! The worst thing is the job was only two weeks old!

"But I got the new job so I wouldn't have to work weekends, just a few hours after school. And now, as soon as I'm done training, they tell me I have to work Fridays! Not just some Fridays—ALL!"

We sit down and listen to her woes. We spend quite a while calming her, encouraging her, and offering alternatives. It's OK, we say, if she doesn't keep this job very long. These after school jobs are not her profession. No, she doesn't have to put them on her résumé some day. We pray together that the Lord will send her a new job, and we encourage her to look.

We begin to read the paper and relax just a bit, when the next teen comes to us brimming with excitement.

"Jim just called! A bunch of us are going to Cedar Point Amusement Park [he names his friends]. AND we're going to invite [he names several girls], and we're going to sleep-over in a van at a campground, and . . ."

"Whoa there, slow down, stop, wait, back up. You're going to WHAT?"

"No, son, you may not go unsupervised overnight with a group of guys and girls."

I tend to say, "No! Forget it. Case closed."

His father says, "Let's think about this for awhile." He asks our teen for more information.

We send the kid in question away while we think. I call another parent to get a more complete picture. I am not surprised when another mom calls to ask, "Did you really give permission for this? We just don't feel right about this mixed group." I assure her that we did not give permission.

Another girl calls saying her parents won't let her go. Why are we not surprised?

We end up calling our son back to us and saying, "These are the choices: You may go with just the guys, or you may all go and come back the same day, or you may choose to stay home." He's going to talk to his friends some more and let us know in a few days. (He ended up going with just guys.)

We finally depart to our various bathrooms to get ready for bed. I just begin to relax under the warm shower when teen number three bursts into the bathroom and wails, "I can't take it anymore! He's suffocating me! I don't have time to talk on the phone constantly, and he calls all the time! Today he called three times!"

THAT DOES IT! I think, "How many crises do we have to handle in one four-hour evening?!"

In desperation to get it over with, I go against my own rules, call the guy myself, tell him my daughter is too young for his constant attentions, and would he please not call anymore? I assure her that it's over and remind her that I usually won't get involved like this; she must set her own limits, etc, etc. I sing her a song and pray, trying to help her relax so she can go to sleep.

My husband and I finally fall into bed and review what we've just concluded with each child to make sure we're "together" on everything. Then, just as we are dozing off, the phone rings. The last young man in question is calling back to assure me that he is an honorable person with only innocent intentions. I tell him I believe him but that our daughter is not interested in his attentions, no matter how honorable. Thank you.

And thank God, this day is over!

All of these things were routine, rather ordinary teenage events, and thankfully, all were quite solvable. But good grief! All in one night?!

◆

Dear Jesus, thank You that You have been with us tonight. Thank You that You have blessed us with children who really want to do the right thing. Thank You for giving us wisdom. In Your name we pray, amen.

58
Security in Boundaries

◆

Hear, my child, your father's instruction, and do not reject your mother's teaching (Proverbs 1:8 NRSV).

My son, do not despise the LORD's discipline and do not resent his rebuke, because the LORD disciplines those he loves, as a father the son he delights in (Proverbs 3:11–12).

I n the book *Successful Step-parenting*, the stepparents Bob and Bonnie Juroe say that sometimes stepchildren will provoke punishment through acts of defiance or misdeeds revolving around the house rules. This may be, they say, because of the child's need to lessen the feelings of abandonment. The child may even be willing to endure pain in order to have the reassurance that the parents will still be there

It was obvious that she hadn't been ready for either the freedom or privilege of driving in the snow, and she gained big-time security from this one particular test of our boundaries.

even when he or she misbehaves. The rationale might be, "I'll find out if my stepparent and parent really care about me. I'll rebel and see what they'll do."*

I believe that any child may do this, "step" or not. By testing the clearly set limits of the family to see what will happen, the kid will find out if the limits are firm. With secure limits the child will feel secure. (Of course there is also security in knowing that exceptions can be discussed and allowances made under special circumstances.)

This was never more evident than at the time we now refer to as "Becky's New Year's Eve Rebellion." One thing that has never gone undisciplined in our family, even from the time of toddlerhood, is the disobedience of a direct and clear instruction. On the night of this story, Becky had had her driver's license only two weeks. She had never driven in snow. All of the kids, except Becky, had plans with friends and so did we.

But nursing colds, we decided at the last minute not to go to our party, and as it turned out, how glad we were! Around nine, our daughter took a phone call and came asking us if she could go see Betty, who was also alone. We weren't thrilled about going out in the cold in order to take her. She said she could drive. The falling snow was very light, and Betty's house was less than two miles away; the drive involved only one intersection.

So we said, "Now, Becky, this is serious. It's New Year's Eve; there are many impaired drivers on the road. Will you solemnly promise to go straight to Betty's house and not go anywhere else?"

"I promise," she said, "and I'll be home by twelve-fifteen."

About and hour and a half later, we got a phone call. Betty's mom was calling from work. "The girls called here about five times begging me to let them go for pizza. I finally caved in, thinking that if you thought Becky could handle it, it must be OK. But the pizza place is on such a busy street, and as I look out, the roads are becoming very snow covered, and I am getting more and more worried. Would you mind going there and following them home?"

"The girl's are WHERE?! No, we don't think she can 'handle it'; she's not experienced enough to go that far on that busy street on a night like this! We did NOT say she could go!"

My husband was out the door so fast I hardly had time to throw on my coat and boots. By now the steady snow covered everything. We arrived at the pizza place and spotted our other car. I waited while Rog went in.

"Hi, Becky."

"Dad!"

"Give me your license."

I took Betty home, and Becky and her dad rode in the other car with quite a conversation going. She was grounded for a month with no license during that time, except for practice sessions with her dad.

We have always said, "Trust and privilege go together." Becky had shown that we couldn't trust her, so she lost her privilege. Others of our kids have had driving privileges rescinded because of jumping in the car and driving off without asking or telling us where. And we have locked up our kids' bikes when they rode after dark without lights or went off without saying where they were going.

All of these things involved disregard for clearly-set family boundaries, and if these rules are allowed to be ignored, there would be no peace, no obedience, and no security for the children in our blended family.

The neatest thing about Becky's New Year's Eve Rebellion is that she and her siblings told the story with glee all around the school! "Hey, you wanna hear the really dumb thing my sister did on New Year's Eve?"

And Becky herself would tell her friends, "No, I can't go with you. I'm grounded. You wanna know why?"

When we ask her why she wasn't embarrassed to tell on herself, she

133

said, "I'm glad I have parents who wouldn't let me get away with something like that. Why, I was so miserable, I never even ate one piece of that pizza!"

She seemed glad that she had parents who wouldn't let her do what she thought she wanted to do. It was obvious that she hadn't been ready for either the freedom or privilege of driving in the snow, and she gained big-time security from this one particular test of our boundaries.

◆

Dear Lord, please continue to make us wise when setting up the boundaries of our family. Help us to know what's important, and give us the strength to consistently enforce the rules we know are good for our children. In Jesus' name and through His power we pray, amen.

*Juroe and Juroe, *Successful Stepparenting,* 55.

59
Letting Go

◆

Train a child in the way that he should go, and when he is old he will not turn from it (Proverbs 22:6).

Now faith is being sure of what we hope for and certain of what we do not see (Hebrews 11:1).

Do not be anxious about anything, but in everything, by prayer and petition, with thanksgiving, present your requests to God. And the peace of God, which transcends all understanding, will guard your hearts and your minds in Christ Jesus (Philippians 4:6–7).

I n the last meditation I talked about family boundaries and the security the children gain from seeing that those boundaries are firm. But it's just as important to know when it's time to remove the boundaries and let our children go. This topic is very difficult for me as we are going through it right now. We are losing two kids at the same time!

I can honestly say in my whole life I have never been so scared. . . . I've never found parenting so hard as this time when I have to stop doing it!

One is going off to college, and the other, although living at home while going to college, is beginning to make choices and decisions about life over which we have no control and with which we may not agree. The latter child is respectful and loving, not immoral or wild by any stretch of the imagination, but still making decisions that make us fearful. We have fought for control at times when it was not appropriate for us to do so. And we have seen the wisdom of letting go of this kid who is quite mature yet so green at living (as we all are the first year out of high school).

For eighteen or nineteen years, we have decided what is best. If we have been afraid or apprehensive for their safety or emotional well-being, we could always say "no." But now we have to back off. Even when we are afraid, we have to say, "the decision is yours."

And with these new freedoms, the time has come for new responsibilities. "You are responsible for your own debts; you are responsible for your own car; it's up to you where you go to school; and yes, based on your financial independence, you may even choose where to live. If you live here, there are some things you will have to abide by, but you will have more freedom than you did in high school." We have tried to prepare them for this time by never giving a privilege without the responsibility. (For example, "If you are going to drive, you have to pay for gas and some insurance.")

But no matter how good a job we've done, it doesn't keep us from being terrified for the adult child that begins to make choices with which we disagree. I can honestly say in my whole life I have never been so scared. I am not afraid because my children aren't ready to be independent—they are. Both of them have proven to be mature and responsible in many ways. But I used to worry when they didn't wear a coat when *I* was cold. Now, they are making decisions about their lives, and I have to let them make the choices, even if I am worried.

A popular talk-show host on Christian radio told how he cried and cried when his son went off to college. When I heard that testimonial, I couldn't believe it. I thought, "How insecure of him! Has he no confidence in his relationship with his child?"

Now I am the one crying. I never thought I would be the type. In the past I thought, "Our home is crowded; how much better it will be when those first two leave!" I've pushed my kids to do things they thought they couldn't do, praised them for their successes, and watched them go off to new jobs and take challenging classes, all of the time thinking that not only they, but I was letting go. And now, when we're down to the wire, when they're really leaving, I feel all sore and broken inside.

I cry easily and find fault easily. Because after all, if they are still bumbling kids, I won't have to let them go! But I have to, because whether I'm ready or not, they are not kids anymore. Whether I read to them enough when they were little, whether I spent enough time listening to them when they were older, whether they've got God's Word in their hearts or not, time is up. They're ready to move on; I gotta let go, and I've never found parenting so hard as this time when I have to stop doing it!

———◆———

Dear Father in heaven, teach me how to let my children go. Please protect and guide them, and may they always obey You, even when they make choices I don't like. In Jesus' name, amen.

60
Sick Kids

◆

Therefore we do not lose heart. Though outwardly we are wasting away, yet inwardly we are being renewed day by day. For our light and momentary troubles are achieving for us an eternal glory that far outweighs them all (2 Corinthians 4:16–17).

I go to the children's school on a snowy morning in the first winter of our marriage. I will watch (I think) enthusiastic third graders put on a Christmas program and eagerly begin the holiday. Andrew has some lines. As I watch his class file in and stand so importantly on the risers in the library, I spot my son, right in the front. And before I have a chance to settle down in pride with that silly, "He's my kid, isn't he

I could make myself sick if I thought about how awful, how possibly twisted her life could have been had we not gotten the healing help that she so desperately needed.

grand?" look on my face, I note with alarm that he is very, very pale. The paleness is definitely more than a case of front-row jitters. His teacher verifies this when she comes to me and whispers, "Andrew says he thinks he's sick, but he's going to try to stick it out."

Before they even sing, while the pianist is playing and people are still arranging themselves, I watch him turn from white to yellow to green! I don't think I ever actually saw someone green before, but green he is and he's my kid!

He sits down suddenly on the stage step. As I hurry to him, I'm thinking, "Thank goodness they haven't started yet." When I get there, it's a quick, "Come on, son," and we flee toward home.

We make it in the door of our nearby (thank goodness!) house, and one second later he's in the bathroom succumbing to the flu.

Our first flu! Will it be an epidemic? As I tuck him in fresh clean sheets on the sofa and settle him with a bucket and a kiss, the phone rings. The school is calling. Becky just threw up on the classroom floor! Poor kid. So back I go.

A short time later, Becky and Andrew are toe to toe (thank goodness our sofa is seven feet long) and looking very pitiful. They also look a bit pleased. It's the first time either of them has been sick with a brother/sister. And busy though it makes me, I'm really glad to be here. They need me. And what they need this day isn't so hard to figure out. Some 7-Up and TLC. A little fussing and they'll be fine.

Not all illnesses are as easy to deal with as the flu. One of my stepchildren had severe symptoms of depression. I had not seen these signs during our courtship, even though we "dated with children" as much as dated alone. But she had gotten into some entrenched patterns of "copping out," and I didn't know what to do.

I decided to inquire about professional help. The wonderful, loving professional with whom I first consulted was also a friend of the family, a friend who had "kept his eye on that girl" and noted her progress and her blossoming and encouraged me to only "keep doing what you're doing." Six months later, I was getting depressed because I couldn't deal with her behavior any more. I recalled Susan's words: "Get help when you think you need it, even if others tell you you don't," so I did.

Thank God it only took a few months of therapy. Some visits were for mom, dad, and daughter. Some were just for stepmom and kid. But most of the time her visits were for her, a time of resolving grief and accepting her new mom. I could make myself sick if I thought about how awful, how possibly twisted, her life could have been had we not gotten the healing help that she so desperately needed.

Recalling all of this reminds me of Harriet, another stepmom, who had to live with even more frustrating and sickening behavior from a stepchild than I did. She and Ben, her new husband, wisely got Mike to a therapist. But unfortunately, the birthmom (who did not have custody) fought them for doing this. Whenever Mike was with his birthmom, she would skip the sessions. Ben took him for awhile, but eventually Mike refused to cooperate because his other mom insisted he didn't have to, and a counselor can't counsel if the client is unwilling. Fortunately, Ben and Harriet had had just enough input from the therapist to follow guidelines and work very very hard at home, and thankfully it worked. Within three years, his sickening and actually filthy behavior had disappeared, and he began to function like a normal, healthy nine-year-old.

I asked Mike's parents to tell me what elements played the most important part in his recovery and improving behavior. They said first of all, the counseling has to be Christian. They spent lots of dollars and wasted lots of time when they tried a counselor that wasn't a Christian. Their second bit of advice was, "Work on the marriage." The kids feel secure when they see love and affection between the couple they live with. When they are secure, they behave better. My friends also said, "Always present a united front." Decide in private what will be a course of action, a discipline, a requirement, and then speak to the child together about it. While it is not possible to agree on everything, absolutely no disagreeing about the child in front of the child!

And the third thing they told me was once you decide on a discipline or requirement, remain firm and consistent. Consistency also breeds security which leads to a happier, more well-adjusted child.

And the final thing they shared: "Have devotions together." God's Word gives strength, wisdom, courage, love. Of all the help we may receive as stepparents, the greatest help comes, as my friends have said, from God and His Word.

So, parents of blended families, to have children who are healthy in body, mind, and spirit, take the advice of my friends: Don't hesitate to get help, keep your marriage strong, be united and consistent in discipline, and daily take time for God together.

◆

Dear Father in heaven, thank You that I get to be the mom of all these kids. Thank You for giving the strength and the time and the love and all it takes to raise them for You. Thank You that I am not a stepmother on my own strength, but that You are my strength. Amen.

61

Joy in All the Children

◆

People were bringing little children to Jesus to have him touch them, but the disciples rebuked them.When Jesus saw this, he was indignant. He said to them, "Let the little children come to me, and do not hinder them, for the kingdom of God belongs to such as these. I tell you the truth, anyone who will not receive the kingdom of God like a little child will never enter it." And he took the children in his arms, put his hands on them and blessed them (Mark 10:13–16).

Yet to all who received him, to those who believed in his name, he gave the right to become children of God—children born not of natural descent, nor of human decision or a husband's will, but born of God (John 1:12–13).

On those special days when I am not feeling the drag of responsibility, I am able to look at each one of my children as the precious and unique gifts from God that they are. Sometimes I could burst with joy when I look at their beauty, hear their wonderful conversations, and see how much they are learning. They are each a wonder, not only of life, but of spiritual and emotional wholeness—a true testimony of God's grace and power in the life of our family.

After all, we must become like little children, Jesus said, to accept the gift of His love. We won't know HOW to be like little children if we don't take time to know what children are like.

You would think that between my birthchildren and stepchildren I have enough kids in my life. But I can't seem to settle for just my own. I want to have special relationships with my nieces and nephews too. Whenever I see them (and it's never enough), I want to hold them, talk to them, learn about them. Aunt Margaret loves Cliffie and Sonya, Emily and Benjamin, Daniel, Nathalie, Tondja, Jessie, Courtney, and Heather.

And as if my own children and my nieces and nephews are not enough, I have to adopt practically the whole neighborhood! The first day I met Timmy, the boy across the street, he was four. He helped me water flowers, and we talked about worms and how we probably shouldn't leave them in the sun to bake but put them back in the cool earth when we're finished looking at them. When I told him this, he told me, "Yes, after all, they are God's creatures too!" Of course I was really impressed with this wisdom. And soon after, his little brother, David, claimed a special place in my heart just because he reminded me of how my own children used to look and act at that age.

Pretty soon his four girl-cousins who live a few doors down began to come by for talks in the yard too. And on their way, why not just include the kids from the houses in-between? So Blake, Derrick, Chelesea, Angela, James, Jordan, and Joseph stop by sometimes too.

The children often come to see if they can "help" when I'm working in my flowers. Of course there's always something they can do! And there are so many things to talk about. Little children are amazing conversationalists—so honest and enthusiastic in the midst of their discovery of life. We have pictures of preschool neighbors licking the beaters my kids got too old to lick, neighbor kids playing in the leaves my kids are raking, and neighborhood kids swimming in our pool.

I know I should be more scholarly; there is so much I need to read if I'm to be a good English teacher. But the children are so awesome! One day little Jesse said, "Look, Mom, there's Maw-gwet. I love Maw-gwet!" Well, Margaret loves Jesse too. And I just have to make time for hugs and front porch chats because each one of these precious little ones needs to know that God loves them and Jesus died for them. And how will they know unless we big people, the ones who teach them about God, love them too?

Jesus was indignant when the disciples wouldn't let the children come. And He would be indignant with me, I think, if I didn't have time to chat with my little friends. Timmy and Jamie and Nikki have already gotten too grown up to come over for a hug, and any year now I know that David and Kelly will be too old too. So while they still feel the freedom of innocence, I will make time to read them a story or have a chat and a hug. After all, we must become like little children, Jesus said, to accept the gift of His love. We won't know *how* to be like little children if we don't take time to know *what* children are like.

———————◆———————

Dear Jesus, thank You for all the special little children in my life. Thank You that I get to be their friend. In Your name, amen.

62
Jealous Children

◆

By wisdom a house is built, and through understanding it is established;
through knowledge its rooms are filled with rare and beautiful treasures
(Proverbs 24:3–4).

So that there should be no division in the body, but that its parts should have
equal concern for each other. If one part suffers, every part suffers with it; if
one part is honored, every part rejoices with it (1 Corinthians 12:25–26).

When Mike and Patty started to date, they were both excited about finding someone who knew how it felt to be deserted by a spouse. They thought they might possibly have found not only a spouse, but a

The behavior stopped of its own accord when the need for the behavior stopped.

stable, sensitive coparent. Freely admitting the mistakes of the past, faithfully committed to God, and with the help of accountability groups for support and change, they thought they could make a "go" of it. But the kids weren't so easily convinced.

Sometimes as they would sit on the front porch talking after the children were in bed, Patty's nine-year-old daughter, Emily, would sit in the upstairs window overlooking the porch and scream. The idea that the one parent she had left might possibly be giving her affections to someone else terrified this child and also made her angry. How could Mom choose someone over her? If Mom loved Mike, then who would love Emily?

How could Emily possibly share her mother's time and affection with a man, let alone with Mike's children as well? Thankfully, Emily got over feeling threatened when Mike spent some special time with her and became her friend too. She was no longer afraid of being deserted. In fact, she actually became glad that she was getting a stepdad.

We had a similar situation. One of the children would pretend to be in pain, "fake" cry, and carry-on something awful when we walked around outside or just the two of us sat talking. First of all we simply had to say, "Stop! You may not carry on like that!" But we also had to reassure her that her dad would always love her, and in fact, I would love and care for her too.

The behavior stopped of its own accord when the *need* for the behavior stopped. As the child gained in security and saw that she wasn't losing a father but was gaining a stepmother, she was able to be more reasonable. She learned from our being together as a family that although she was not the center of the universe and would not be singled out for extra attention, EACH of our children would be treated as special at certain times. And so would she.

She would be expected to give as much to family relationships as the other children, and she would receive as much attention as the other kids. If we had given her more time and attention, we would have fed into her selfishness and attempts to manipulate. But treating her fairly, as another one of all special children in the family, she gained in security.

One of the ways I made each child feel special in the first year or so of our marriage was to have a "kid of honor day." On this day, the honored child would pick the supper menu (from choices offered by me), have a special place-setting at the table, maybe even have a small gift, and we would sing "For He/She's a Jolly Good Fellow." This honor could be for the end of a ball season, doing great on a school project, learning to tie shoelaces, getting the coveted part in the play, the first baby-sitting job well done, etc.

Any little accomplishment at all can be an excuse to honor a kid. (Pay attention to not honoring the same one twice before honoring them each at least once!) After a time, this tradition died out. We have plenty of birthdays to celebrate, and on that day we all honor the individual. But when the children were younger and birthdays seemed very far apart for them, the "kid of honor" meals were very helpful in making each of our children feel loved, secure, and special.

◆

Dear Father in heaven, thank You for wisdom in raising these children and blending our family. Thank You that each one is special, and may all of our children know that they are special both to You and to us.
In Jesus' name, amen.

63

Biting and Devouring or Serving in Love

◆

You . . . were called to be free. But do not use your freedom to indulge the
sinful nature; rather, serve one another in love. The entire law is summed up in
a single command: "Love your neighbor as yourself." If you keep on biting and
devouring each other, watch out or you will be destroyed by each other
(Galatians 5:13–15).

The people who live in our house would all agree that one of the worst things about living in a blended family is simply being crowded. The fighting that sometimes accompanies the reality of shared living space seems a lot like "biting and devouring." The Scripture verse reminds me of that nursery rhyme:

Lack of privacy is again found to be the "main pain." Thinking in a loving way about each other can lead to more positive thinking in everything.

> There once were two cats of Kilkenny,
>   Each thought there was one cat too many;
> So they fought and they fit,
>   And they scratched and they bit,
> Till excepting their nails
>   And the tips of their tails,
> Instead of two cats, there weren't any.

I have a hunch the mother who made this up was sick of seeing and hearing her children scrap over space and dominance in their home! At those times each kid thinks there are "too many," and of course each wants to be the only one.

The boys divide their room with tall bookshelves. But their music still clashes, and the light of the night owl still bothers the one who wants to go to bed earlier. The girls, whose room is undivided except for a general "your side and my side," complain of the other's waking them up, the other's messes, and the most horrid thing of all—"She's wearing my clothes!"

Mom's office is a corner of the basement which is already overflowing with exercise equipment, laundry, gerbils, books, and Sega paraphernalia.

In all of this, the challenge is learning to love one another and serve one another rather than "biting and devouring each other." Space invasion and the violation of property rights can lead to destructive arguments between not only teens, but teens and parents as well. So we can set limits such as: "Watch what you say!" "You may not unlock a locked door." "Knock first." "Ask permission to use anything not yours." "Put everything you use back where you got it." We can learn to respect each other, and by serving one another in love, we can make our big family something desirable rather than something negative.

For us, serving each other in love in a big family means there is always someone to talk to and to talk things over with. There is always a peer who will answer, "How does this look?" or "How does this work?" or "Give me a hand with this, will you?" or "Can you give me a ride?" or "Will you go with me?" But it also means not using another's stuff, keeping shared spaces picked up, doing one's share of the work.

Thinking in a loving way about each other can lead to more positive thinking in everything. For example, to think more lovingly about my home may mean that rather than feeling annoyance at our limited space, I need to focus on what we have in our home that we can use together. I can think about how lovely our home is, our pool, our beautiful lawn and garden. And there ARE pluses in a smaller house, such as we can clean it all in very little time; as I work in my crowded basement "office," I can still hear and see most of what is going on; we are close enough to communicate back and forth but far enough away that a closed door usually works for at least a limited time of privacy.

The bottom line is choosing how we will think. Will we focus on the noise, mess, and annoyance of so many? Or will we think about the love we share and the time we have with one another?

We must teach our children how to think and act lovingly—not like cats that scratch and bite and devour one another.

◆

Dear Father in heaven, please help us not to bite and devour one another. Rather than fighting for preeminence, may we serve one another in love. Thank You for Your Spirit that empowers us. In Jesus' name, amen.

64
Never Enough Money

◆

But godliness with contentment is great gain. For we brought nothing into the world, and we can take nothing out of it. But if we have food and clothing, we will be content with that. People who want to get rich fall into temptation and a trap and into many foolish and harmful desires that plunge men into ruin and destruction. For the love of money is a root of all kinds of evil. Some people, eager for money, have wandered from the faith and pierced themselves with many griefs (1 Timothy 6:6–10).

Peter answered: "May your money perish with you, because you thought you could buy the gift of God with money! You have no part or share in this ministry, because your heart is not right before God. Repent of this wickedness and pray to the Lord. Perhaps he will forgive you for having such a thought in your heart. For I see that you are full of bitterness and captive to sin"
(Acts 8:20–23).

When asked what he thought was the worst thing about living in a blended family, one of the children said, "It's just the pits that there are so many kids; there is not enough money for everything I want." This answer makes me realize just why God hasn't allowed us to be one of the families to win a sweepstakes! After all, we really have so much.

When I stopped complaining and started asking God for wisdom, instead of showing us how we could afford a bigger house, He showed me how to make better use of the one we have.

We have a nice house, three cars (one for the kids to drive), the kids go to a Christian school, we take a vacation some years, and we can afford to send the children to camp, youth conventions, and youth-group work trips. And we do take weekend getaways together.

What I'm saying is, we can afford lots of things beyond the necessary food, clothing, and shelter; therefore, we should be content. But this particular kid looks at the bigger houses of people we know, at people who go south every spring break, at people who wear designer clothing or give their kids spending money instead of making them earn it, and of course he would like those things for us as well. But what good would it really do? For as the verse above says, you cannot buy the gifts of God with money.

What God wants is not for us to have the easiest life possible, but for each one of us to be developed into the character that He desires for us. Love, joy, peace, patience, kindness, gentleness, and self-control are from the Spirit (Galatians 5:22), and no amount of money can increase our love for one another or bring us peace and happiness.

The first verse above says, "if we have food and clothing, we will be content with that." The word "will" makes me think of an act of the will. I had to learn contentment by an act of my will. I was so frustrated with the crowdedness of our home a few years ago, I thought I would go nuts. We looked around at bigger houses, but it was definitely not a good time for us to buy and exchange our nice easy mortgage for a bigger, more burdensome one.

I prayed and agonized over this issue and complained a lot! But in the end God gave me wisdom. I was able to completely change the way we use the rooms we have. By doing some major rearranging, I was able to get several more feet of living space out of the living room and a whole additional cupboard in the kitchen. It was a miracle! I got more space by simply making better use of what I already had.

I had complained and agonized, begged and even coveted. When I stopped complaining and started asking God for wisdom, instead of showing us how we could afford a bigger house, He showed me how to make better use of the one we have. I never would have thought it possible, but it's true. For the past year now, I have been so happy with our home that even after touring a huge house (seven bedrooms) of another blended family, I honestly would not trade ours for it! They are so spread out! How do they even know where all the children are?

After much complaining, I willed to be content, and God brought me contentment. I am praying that our discontented child will learn that godliness with contentment is great gain.

◆

Dear God, the Provider, the All-Sufficient One, thank You for all that You have provided for us. Thank You for giving me wisdom to use my home well, and thank You for all the good things that You have given us. In Jesus' name, amen.

65
So Many Relatives

◆

Dear friends, let us love one another, for love comes from God. Everyone who loves has been born of God and knows God. Whoever does not love does not know God, because God is love. . . . Dear friends, since God so loved us, we also ought to love one another. No one has ever seen God; but if we love each other, God lives in us and his love is made complete in us
(1 John 4:7–8,11–12).

I sometimes view the big extended family of our blended family as a negative. There are so many Christmas get-togethers, so many holiday demands, that the feeling of being torn accompanies most family gatherings. Every older person wants to see us and talk to us more than is humanly possible. For example, we have five grandmothers, and rather than just enjoying loving them all, I sometimes think of them as a responsibility to

The worst thing about living in a blended family is having so many people in your family, and the best thing about living in a blended family is having so many people in your family!

be met. If we were to see each grandmother once a month on a "free-day" (of which there is really no such thing), we would not have enough weeks in the month to see them all! And yet, what a support group they are! A problem needs prayer? Call the grandmas!

While the blended, extended family can be a burden and a hassle, and definitely limits our social life with friends, if you ask the children, this will probably be the thing they say they like the most. The girls love having the extra, younger aunts. Their birthmother's sisters are more like grandmothers to them, but my sisters are younger than I, giving the girls more "cool" young adults in their lives. They can borrow party dresses, talk about dating with someone who has recent experiences, and enjoy my sisters' younger families. Rog's brothers, most younger than he, provide the same type of enrichment for the boys.

All the kids love the huge family get-togethers on Rog's and his first wife's sides of the family. There are more people than we can possibly know well, but it's interesting and fun for all the kids to try. One son loves to sit and chat with the teachers and preachers that seem to abound in those families; the other son always finds someone with a unique car to check out or a gang who wants to shoot baskets with him.

So while Mom may worry and feel pressured with pleasing and visiting beloved grannies and aunts, the kids are enjoying the crowd and growing in security. Being part of these huge groups is part of who they are as individuals and who we are as a family. As one of our daughters put it, "The worst thing about living in a blended family is having so many people in your family, and the best thing about living in a blended family is having so many people in your family!"

◆

Dear Lord, thank You for all the ways that You enrich our lives through others. Thank You for our big, big extended family and every relative that adds enrichment to our blended family. In Jesus' name, amen.

66

The Lost Position of the Stepchild

◆

Love must be sincere. Hate what is evil; cling to what is good. Be devoted to one another in brotherly love. Honor one another above ourselves. Never be lacking in zeal, but keep your spiritual fervor, serving the Lord. Be joyful in hope, patient in affliction, faithful in prayer (Romans 12:9–12).

Dear friends, since God so loved us, we also ought to love one another (1 John 4:11).

There is a saying among counselors, "The stepfamily is born of loss." Even as we come together to love and support one another through life, the loss is always a part of who we are and what made us into our very special kind of family. For a child, that loss may include not only the loss of a parent and the loss of a nuclear family, but also the loss of a specific position in the family.

> *No matter how much you love your children and stepchildren, the more children there are, the more they have to share the limelight and individual attention.*

Rather than despairing over the "lost position," a child can learn, with your help, to embrace his or her new position. Just as they had to accept the loss of the nuclear family as part of the pain and growth process of their lives, they can learn that this adjustment of where they fit in the family is part of what is making them into the person God wants them to be.

One man raised in a blended family told me, "I lost my place in the family and I never got it back." But immediately he explained that that situation had specifically led to personal and spiritual growth.

I know the parents behind his experience, and they attempted to treat him and the stepsibling equally, more or less as twins. While they thought he shared equally in his position, he felt he did not. As he explained further, I understood that no matter how much you love your children and stepchildren, the more children there are, the more they have to share the limelight and individual attention. Perhaps they even understand that they are better off with two parents, while at the same time coveting the position they had when there were fewer kids and they were the "only oldest" or the "only baby."

Kevin Leman gives some practical advice concerning birth order in his book, *How to Live in a Stepfamily Without Getting Stepped On.* He tells parents that they need to remember, "When a child who is born into one birth order lands in another position in his blended family, do not treat the child as something he is not. He may have to take on different responsibilities or play different roles at times, but never forget who he really is."*

If "the baby" has always done less work than the other kids, of course give him work, but don't suddenly expect him to live up to the responsibilities of a middle child just because that is his position in the new family. And if the oldest has always had special privileges, remember that child still needs to be treated in a special way, even if it means sharing that "specialness" with someone else.

If the expectations for the child change too much or if the "specialness" seems to have totally vanished, the child may resent the stepsiblings and perhaps the marriage. While you can't change the birth order of the children that live together, note their place in the family. A stepparent can listen and love the child who may feel robbed of specialness. If feelings are hurt, even if you can't understand, simply care. Be there for the child; try to see things from his or her point of view, and tell him or her it's OK to feel bad.

If your child has invited Christ to live within, you can challenge them from the Scripture. Lovingly and gently teach them. With the help of verses such as those above, they can learn from the example of Jesus Christ. The second verse above is from the following passage: "This is love: not that we loved God, but that he loved us and sent his Son as an atoning sacrifice for our sins. Dear friends, since God so loved us, we also ought to love one another. No one has ever seen God; but if we love each other, God lives in us and his love is made complete in us" (1 John 4:10–12). Even in the midst of feeling displaced (which, by the way, they won't be feeling every single minute), they can still learn to act in a loving and caring way toward one another when Christ with His supernatural love dwells within.

◆

Dear God, wise and loving Parent that You are, please teach us of Your wisdom and give us Your love as we nurture and love our children. May we be able to love our children and stepchildren unconditionally, even if we don't understand how they may feel. No matter what other things our children feel, may they feel loved. In Jesus' name, amen.

---

*Kevin Leman, *Living in a Stepfamily Without Getting Stepped On*, 23.

67
Exercise for Body, Mind, and Soul

◆

...train yourself to be godly. For physical training is of some value, but godliness has value for all things, holding promise for both the present life and the life to come (1 Timothy 4:7b–8).

Everyone who competes in the games goes into strict training. They do it to get a crown that will not last; but we do it to get a crown that will last forever. Therefore I do not run like a man running aimlessly; I do not fight like a man beating the air. No, I beat my body and make it my slave so that after I have preached to others, I myself will not be disqualified for the prize (1 Corinthians 9:25–27).

Becky is really into working out. She jogs almost every day and works through a collection of toning exercises. She has picked out a "look" for her arms and is working toward it by doing certain "body sculpting" exercises. I admire her discipline and praise her for her new fitness. With regular exercise, she has a much more positive outlook on life and looks great too.

After about a year of watching my children get into physical shape, I wondered, Have they been working out their minds and spirits as well as their bodies?

Then there is Andrew. He is thin like his two parents who were beanpole adolescents. But he won't be satisfied with it anymore, oh no! His name means "man of strength," and he is determined that that is what he will be. Although still thin, his new body look is one of defined muscles. The muscles in his arms, his neck, and his shoulders are defined by long, lean, clearly outlined bulges. Though he has been working out for a long time, I am just now realizing that I can call on him to lift heavy things. Now my son says, "Mom, please, get out of the way! I can do this by myself. (Geesh-mutter-mutter.) Do you think I'm still a kid?" I am proud of both Andrew and Becky because all of this fitness has come about by discipline and hard work.

But after about a year of watching my children get into physical shape and become more and more preoccupied with such things, I wondered, Have they been working out their minds and spirits as well as their bodies? Using the above verses, we had a talk about being balanced people. As the verse says, "physical training has some value."

In our family we are very aware that we need exercise for good health. I know that I don't sleep well unless I get in my daily walk or swim, and more than once in my life I have pulled myself out of depression with exercise and nutrition. I also must exercise daily for cardiac health. But no matter how fit we are, in the end our bodies will fail us. They are, after all, just a temporary dwelling place for our souls. We must not neglect our souls.

I have encouraged these two kids to read. Some pretty interesting teen devotional books have circulated through our family. And all the kids can recall at least one book that they really liked some time in their lives.

So I encourage a little, bribe a little, and, yes, nag because some of us by nature tend toward mind things, and some toward things of the body. Both have value. (I nag my other kids to get out there and exercise!) But we know that it is the spiritual things that will last. I would like to challenge you, as I have my children, to always grow in body, mind, and spirit.

A good book, always in process, is a wonderful way to grow the mind. There is no place you cannot go or anybody you cannot be if you read. There is no limit to how much reading can broaden your understanding of others, of God, and of the world around you. You don't have to sit down and devour a book from cover to cover; modern life is not usually conducive to that style. But a few pages a night can get you through a quality book in a few months or even a year.

Someone I love very much suffered brain damage from exposure to toxic chemicals in her office building. She brought herself back by reading just one or two pages of a good book each night. She couldn't believe the hope and peace that came to her as even for those few minutes she felt herself exercising her mind. She read a short devotional, maybe one verse of Scripture, each morning to actively keep her heart and soul together in the midst of her crisis. Then at night she read the one or two pages of a book. Each of these activities took less than five minutes, but they were marvelously mind and heart changing, thought improving, hope-filled moments for her.

Grow yourself. Exercise your mind, exercise your body, and nourish your soul every day from God's Word.

◆

Dear Creator God, thank You for the way You made us: body, mind, and soul. Thank You for life and new life in Christ Jesus. Help us to tend to our life, both physical and spiritual, and keep ourselves growing every day and in every way. In Jesus' name and for Your glory, amen.

68

Encouragement for the Race

◆

Therefore, since we are surrounded by such a great cloud of witnesses, let us throw off everything that hinders us and the sin that so easily entangles, and let us run with perseverance the race marked out for us. Let us fix our eyes on Jesus, the author and perfecter of our faith, who for the joy set before him endured the cross, scorning its shame, and sat down at the right hand of the throne of God. Consider him who endured such opposition from sinful men, so that you will not grow weary and lose heart (Hebrews 12:1–3).

Picture, says the author of Hebrews, an Olympic race. For a long-distance competition, the runners run around the stadium many times while a huge crowd in surrounding stands watches. Perhaps we have excitedly become as one with the mass of humanity witnessing the event, like a great cloud around the runners, yelling, cheering them on to the goal.

Their coaches and some of the announcers are previous Olympic runners themselves. Their very presence speaks, "I did it, and you can do it too! I broke the record before you; you can break mine! Come on, you can do it!" And they do.

The idea of becoming fully who I am, the completed and perfected person that God created me to be—with no more battle against sin, no weakness, no fatigue in my flesh or in my spirit—this is something that inspires me onward even now.

They win by fixing their eyes on the goal and running with perseverance the race marked out for them. They have trained well, probably for years, honing their bodies, getting rid of every weakness and every bit of flab that could hold them back or weigh them down. Clothes are worn that do not bind or inhibit in any way. They run the race, and some of them win.

Likewise, says the author of Hebrews, run your race faithfully for God. For generations, men and women of faith, some of them martyred, have run the race faithfully before us, showing us that we can win. Their spirits join with the crowd around us, cheering us on, saying, "Yes, it can be done. You can run the race; live this life faithfully and reach everlasting glory."

So let us strip off anything that slows us down or holds us back in the Christian life—especially sins that may so easily trip us up and cause us to take our sights off Jesus. He is both the originator and goal of our race. Forgetting what is behind, press on toward the goal of being made like Christ, perfected in glory.

The Greek winner got a crown of olive leaves. A modern winner gets a gold, silver, or bronze medal. The Christian who wins receives "the crown of life" (James 1:12). This is a symbol for everlasting life, the life of one who is wholly perfected and lives eternally united with God in heaven.

I may have a "nice life" here on earth. Perhaps I don't long for heaven as I would if my life were not so nice, if I were very poor or more persecuted or suffering. But the idea of becoming fully who I am, the completed and perfected person that God created me to be—with no more battle against sin, no weakness, no fatigue in my flesh or in my spirit—this is something that inspires me onward even now. To have all the old marks of sin gone, to be like Christ, that is the goal. And in the very presence of God I will lose all awareness of myself and be totally taken up with worship and praise to Him, my Creator, my Lifegiver. He brings me earthly life; He brings life to my spirit.

———————◆———————

Dear Creator God, thank You for life. Empower me by Your Spirit to faithfully run the race of my life. Help me to confess any sin—the love of material things, self-indulgent pleasures, or anything that would keep me from focusing on You and becoming like You. Thank You for the great number of saints in the flesh who encourage me on and for the ones from the past who inspire me by their examples to run this race and win.
In the mighty name of Jesus I pray, amen.

69
Blessed Quietness

◆

"Be still, and know that I am God; I will be exalted among the nations, I will be exalted in the earth" (Psalm 46:10).

Those whom I love I rebuke and discipline. So be earnest, and repent. Here I am! I stand at the door and knock. If anyone hears my voice and opens the door, I will come in and eat with him, and he with me (Revelation 3:19–20).

Peace I leave with you; my peace I give you. I do not give to you as the world gives. Do not let your hearts be troubled and do not be afraid (John 14:27).

Leaning back in the chair at my computer, I close my eyes and hungrily absorb the fresh quietness of the house. The kids are back in school! Even though they are all teenagers, have jobs, and are busy with friends all summer, there

All summer long I clung to my worries, nursed my hurts, fed my anger, and ignored His Word.

is something different about knowing the house will be empty for seven hours, something different from the smaller periods of an empty house in summer. Knowing they are safe at school and probably not expecting anything from me for awhile allows me to relax.

On the first morning they are back in school, the quietness seems deeper, the air seems lighter. Ideas flow uninterrupted through my brain. I turn my thinking to God's Word. Poignant promises, hearty exhortations, and verses of passionate worship come to mind, refreshing my spirit and restoring my soul. I feel my nerves and my body relax. This is peace.

There are many opportunities for quiet and peace both outside and inside of me, however, that I do not take. God calls, "Be still and know Me," but there are things I allow in the way. Sometimes I am angry. Instead of "God thoughts" that bring refreshment and renewal, I get a bit of quietness and use it to think, "Why did she . . . ? Why doesn't he ever learn? He makes me so mad when he . . . How could she do that? . . . say that? Of all the nerve! What a brat!"

And where do these thoughts get me? Into a grouchy, angry mood when the family does regather. I could take a moment to let the Spirit bring rest and peace to my soul, but instead I nurse irritation and aggravation until I am tense and restless for days.

Another mini-moment of peace and quiet is interrupted by anxiety. "Where is that kid? What is he doing now? He knows we need the car here, he didn't even ask! When will he learn? Oh dear, she's going to be late for work. What could be keeping him? What if he got in an accident? She shouldn't be out so late. Doesn't she know we worry? She sees way too much of that guy. Is she safe?"

Another moment of peace that could have been my soul's refreshment is lost to anxiety and fear. God calls me, "Cease your striving! I'm God!" But I don't hear because I'm not listening. I know better. I know that there are tons of powerful reassuring verses in God's Word. But for some reason I cling to my anxiety. I know I should be "casting all your care upon him; for he careth for you" (1 Peter 5:7 KJV), yet I'm not doing it, choosing instead to wallow in worry.

After weeks of such turmoil, of little rest for my body or soul, I finally begin to feed tiny bits of God's Word into my mind. I'm like a person who has been very ill, and I take in only a little food at first. And behold, my strength of mind and heart begins to return!

As I give my children over to God, as I learn to live with their independence from me, my peace returns. By the time the first day of school comes, I have been cleansed from my negative thinking and sinful thoughts. I am ready for an encounter that still surprises me when it happens. And as I lean back in my chair, I hear Him clearly say, "Be still and know that I am God," and once again I know it. Now that I am listening to Him again, when quiet comes to my house, He is in it, and the moment washes over me with oceans of love and waves of peace.

All the time God had been calling to me, "Enough! Cease your striving, for I am God!" But I held on to the anger and anxiety, and it roared so loudly in my heart I couldn't hear Him. All summer long I clung to my worries, nursed my hurts, fed my anger, and ignored His Word. But when I couldn't take the fatigue of worry anymore, when I couldn't stand the tension of anger another minute, I was ready to start changing my heart with His Word. How much His Word means to me; it is heavy with promises, blazing with power!

◆

Exalted One, I praise You. I give You honor and glory and praise for calling me even when I wasn't listening. Thank You for never ceasing to knock on the door of my heart. May we eat together of Your Word, may our fellowship continue uninterrupted. For Your glory I pray in the name of Jesus, amen.

70

Too Busy to Listen

◆

Be still, and know that I am God (Psalm 46:10a).

She had a sister called Mary, who sat at the Lord's feet listening to what he said. But Martha was distracted by all the preparations that had to be made. She came to him and asked, "Lord, don't you care that my sister has left me to do the work by myself? Tell her to help me!" "Martha, Martha," the Lord answered, "you are worried and upset about many things, but only one thing is needed. Mary has chosen what is better, and it will not be taken away from her" (Luke 10:39–41).

As a busy mom who has always done a lot of entertaining, this Scripture presents a very difficult lesson for me. Even as a child listening to this story in Sunday school, no matter how hard I tried to understand, I would always

The Lord God was there in the flesh, and Martha was too busy to listen!

be on Martha's side! I am a reader, a lover of books, and someone who knows the importance of a "quiet time" each day. I love lingering after a meal and discussing theology, doctrine, theatre, books, etc. But for me it has always been, "See to everyone's needs first. Make your guests feel welcome, feed everyone, care for everyone, and THEN you may have the pleasure of quiet listening to the Lord." The time of quiet listening rarely comes.

This Scripture tells me I'm wrong. The Lord God was there in the flesh, and Martha was too busy to listen! You bet I'd be busy too! If the Lord came to my house for dinner, I'd be run ragged, using the best china, making sure everything was not only edible but had great eye appeal, and I would be snapping at my kids to help get the meal on. When I read this, I wonder, Wasn't Jesus hungry? If he had indeed come for dinner, who would put the food on if Martha didn't?

My Bible commentary says that the words indicate Martha's preparations had her "worrying anxiously," and that if she had "lightened up"—not insisted on such an elaborate meal but gone with something more simple—she wouldn't have been so harried. There is something to be said, apparently, for knowing when to serve sandwiches on paper plates, for knowing what suits the occasion.

These commentators suggest that these sisters represent *two good* ways of serving the Lord. But Martha's service will die with her while Mary's service will never end. Both were true-hearted disciples, but while one was absorbed in the contemplative, the other was involved in the active style of honoring the Lord. "A church full of Marys," says the commentary, "would perhaps be as great an evil as a church full of Marthas!"* Both are needed to complement the other.

I like those comments. It allows me to be both Mary and Martha in my character at different times. The younger my family, the more I have HAD to be a "Martha." I accepted this role easily. Being the oldest girl in a large family, I always had to care about the "preparations." But a big part of me has always wanted to be more of a "Mary" too, and I am extremely grateful for this current stage of my life in which I can choose this way more often.

Having said that, it isn't easy to switch roles. This difficulty can be illustrated by a recent weekend with my son. A favorite aunt and uncle of mine invited us to their retirement home for a golfing weekend. She is a champion entertainer and gourmet cook; he is a consummate golfer. My grandma was there too, and the two women are very accustomed to working together. But of course I felt that I had to help. I felt guilty being waited on, didn't want them to work too hard on my behalf, and kept asking, "What can I do?" Finally, I just "lightened up" and enjoyed their hospitality. It was wonderful to be the guest for a change! By accepting what they were doing for me, I actually made what they were trying to do easier. When it was time to go, I was so enjoying being waited on I didn't want to leave! I am learning, however gradually, to be both a Martha and a Mary.

———————◆———————

Dear Lord Jesus, help me to come more often and sit at Your feet. Thank You that You came to this earth as God incarnate and allowed women to sit at Your feet, learning of You and worshiping in the most personal of ways. Thank You for all my years as Martha. Help me now to be more like Mary and more consistently choose what is better. In Your name, amen.

Commentary on the Whole Bible, Jamieson, Fausset and Brown, eds., (Grand Rapids: Zondervan, 1976), 1005.

71

Love Talk

◆

The husband should fulfill his marital duty to his wife, and likewise the wife to her husband. The wife's body does not belong to her alone but also to her husband. In the same way, the husband's body does not belong to him alone but also to his wife. Do not deprive each other except by mutual consent and for a time, so that you may devote yourselves to prayer (1 Corinthians 7:3–5a).

How beautiful you are, my darling! Oh, how beautiful! Your eyes are doves (Song of Songs 1:15).

How handsome you are, my lover! Oh, how charming! And our bed is verdant (Song of Songs 1:16).

My lover spoke and said to me, "Arise my darling, my beautiful one, and come with me. See! The winter is past; the rains are over and gone. Flowers appear on the earth; the season of singing has come. . . . Arise, come my darling; my beautiful one, come with me." (Song of Songs 2:10–13)

Oh, wow! Many of us may wish that our husband or wife would speak such wonderful love poetry to us. But the truth is, most of us are not as poetic as the lovers in the Song of Songs. (You can, however, read this beautiful book to

> *A few kind words, which cost absolutely nothing, can stir up feelings of love.*

one another!) The important thing is not how poetical you sound, but that you do, as lovers, have a love language—body language and verbal cues that tell the other person you love them and want them. I'm not just talking about preparing for sex. We all have a need to feel desired, wanted, cared for, and cherished. Speaking lovingly to one another helps create these feelings in a relationship.

One of you may feel more comfortable expressing romance than the other. For instance, neither Jack nor Jill is good at romancing each other. (Sometimes I wonder how they even got together!) But they have love and feelings of affection for one another, so they have actually been seeking counseling and reading books to teach them how to express love, how to speak kindly and lovingly to one another. They are learning that it begins with simple kindness and goes on to words and gestures of affection.

I have said before that being "in love" in our culture is often considered a helpless state over which you have no control. But if you regularly tell your mate you appreciate him or her, feelings of affection WILL steadily grow. For example, "That was a good meal, dear, thank you." Or, "Thanks for fixing that leaking faucet. When you care for our home, you make me feel cherished and cared for too." Especially applicable to a blended family situation is, "You know, when you do something special for my kid, it makes me feel really warm towards you! Thanks for taking the time." A few kind words, which cost absolutely nothing, can stir up feelings of love.

The unexpected flowers, the encouraging phone call in the middle of a frustrating day, the little pat as you pass by, a shoulder rub, a hug, a kiss at the door, all of these things are simple kindnesses that can stir feelings of passion. Then, as things really heat up, don't forget to keep talking! It is wonderful when two sagging, middle-aged people can say to each other, "I love your body!" "I love the way your skin feels." "Your scent really turns me on." Again, just words—words that anyone can say, but when directed toward your mate, they can turn that mate into an object of desire.

I believe kind, affectionate, and sexy words are even more important in a second marriage, especially after the honeymoon glow has worn off. When the passion cools, as it always does at some point, you may begin to wonder how you measure up to the first spouse. You will never have to wonder, not even for a moment, if your spouse speaks to you in the way described above.

When the emotional warmth of the first marriage was extinguished, the sexual intimacy in the marriage died as well. Now you are married a second time, and everything seems glorious, especially the physical relationship.

But when the reality of each of your imperfections begins to appear more often than your joy at finding each other, it is time to begin the careful nurturing of your love. Intentionally practice kindness; purpose to say one or two kind and loving things each day to your spouse, especially words of appreciation, and watch the fire of passion not only stay kindled but burn brightly!

———————◆———————

Help me, Lord, to be genuinely kind and loving toward my spouse. Remove the familial and cultural barriers that may make me feel inhibited, and help me to speak words of affection and appreciation. Help me to be able to show and tell my mate how much he/she means to me every day. Thank You for our marriage, Lord, and may we always nurture our love. In Your name and for Your glory we pray, amen.

72
Nobody's Perfect

◆

Not that I have already obtained all this, or have already been made perfect,
but I press on to take hold of that for which Christ Jesus took hold of me
(Philippians 3:12).

But the Lord stood at my side and gave me strength, so that through me the
message might be fully proclaimed . . . And I was delivered from the lion's
mouth. The Lord will rescue me from every evil attack and will bring me
safely to his heavenly kingdom. To him be glory for ever and ever. Amen
(2 Timothy 4:17–18).

When I suddenly had girls in addition to my two little boys, I was glad. Now, I thought, I get to do hair, use ribbons and bows, buy dresses, anklets, and lace. It was so much fun. But along with the fun was the tense realization that everyone in Rog's world, the world I had married into, was watching. When our newly blended family would walk into church, descend the aisle, and file into our seats, I knew that everyone, at least in those first weeks, was checking us out.

I screamed, "I can't stand this anymore!! Shut up! Shut up! Shut up!". . . I feared the new people in my life would value me only if I did a perfectly good job of being a step-mother. I doubted their willingness to accept me for me.

Some people looked for everything to be neat, clean, and organized. (That we usually managed.) Others looked for perfectly coordinated outfits and nicely done hair. Sometimes this happened, and, as you can imagine, with seven people it often did not. A few old ladies bobbed their heads in approval at the matching headbands with bows that accompanied each girl's new dress. But I worried, did anyone notice that Lisa had on one tall sock and one medium height sock, both pulled up way higher than they should be? (I thought I would NEVER get that girl to be neat about the details!) And someone else's hair didn't turn out, and some guy had on the wrong socks, and someone else's pants weren't quite clean. And a few people (now friends who admit it to me) looked to see if we were wearing any designer labels! Others were reassured to find out that our clothes still came from the same department stores theirs did.

162

After exerting tremendous amounts of effort to make us look picture perfect (and we seldom could be as perfect as I pictured), then came the standards for behavior. If anyone was naughty, if anyone snubbed an adult who greeted them, if anyone didn't behave, if anyone sassed me in front of other people, they knew "You're dead for a week. Don't even try it!" And when someone did transgress, oh wow! Be sure Mom would get in the car and say, "I'd like to see you in the bedroom as soon as we get home."

After a few weeks of continual Sunday-morning-aiming-for-perfection angst, I went to Ladies Bible Study. When I walked in, the speaker for the night came up and asked me if I could share a story from my day about being angry. She wanted to illustrate reasons we get angry and was looking for volunteers to share various kinds of angry incidents. Without worrying about it too much I said, "Sure."

When it was my turn, I told how frustrated I had been that day when my five elementary-school-age kids, all at one time, were talking at me. No one was willing to wait their turn; I was trying to get supper on, and all five demanded attention at once or picked on each other under my feet. I got mad, I said. I ran into the living room, knelt in a high-backed chair, and pounding the back of that chair as hard and fast as my fists could fly, I screamed, "I can't stand this anymore!! Shut up! Shut up! Shut up!"

Some ladies laughed, a few nodded their heads, and when I realized what I had given away, I got embarrassed and afraid. This was a cultural subgroup of women known for their "supermoms." I had heard more than one person say, "You haven't been mothered unless you've had a Dutch mother." And I had talked to a few moms who just seemed to be so perfectly nurturing, so totally unselfish, so slavish to their children that I felt inferior whenever I was in their presence. What had I done, revealing myself like this? And those supermoms may have been listening! My own husband, when he heard about my afternoon, rather than having sympathy and understanding, had been quite appalled by my behavior. Now all these women knew how emotional I was!

When we went to our discussion groups to talk about the lecture, I told my small group how I had embarrassed myself and, feeling like such a bad mother, wished I hadn't told. One of the women my age whom I admired and who already knew me fairly well, said, "Are you kidding? I was relieved to find out you weren't perfect!" (And I had thought *she* was one of the "sainted ones"!) Others chimed in with, "Nobody's perfect," and "I've yelled the same thing myself."

Each of them unloaded tales of bad days, impossible kids, and various miserable stages they all go through. When we were done sharing, I felt perfectly normal! Then we shared about the power of prayer, God's strength in our weakness, and we promised to pray for each other.

This, along with realistic conversations with a new friend and another dear older saint who constantly praised and encouraged me, changed my attitude. I stopped trying to have a perfect family and instead tried before God to do the best I could. That means that some friends still think I'm too perfect, and others feel like I should still try harder.

What Kevin Leman says in his book, *Living in a Stepfamily Without Getting Stepped On,* is so true: "Rare is the stepfamily in which a stepparent isn't criticized. If you're seeking perfectionism, you will hate the criticism (and probably the critics). If you're seeking excellence, you're more apt to welcome criticism. You may not enjoy it, but you can accept it and learn from it."*

I've seen firsthand that having a perfectionistic attitude set me up for self-doubt and misery. I feared the new people in my life would value me only if I did a perfectly good job of being a stepmother. I doubted their willingness to accept me for me. Every failure depressed me and made me feel inferior. But when I learned to settle for less than perfection, I could accept failure (messy kids, never having a neat house) much more easily. Not that I give up trying! Not me! But rather than being devastated by the inability to be perfect, I can now be encouraged by wherever we succeed and whenever we are an excellent family.

◆

Dear God, help me to keep in mind the most important things, like loving You and loving each other. Help me to worry less about appearances and more about the condition of my heart. Help me to love my children even when they are unlovely. In Your name, amen.

---

*Kevin Leman, *Living in a Stepfamily Without Getting Stepped On*, 60.

73
Blending in Marriage

◆

"Haven't you read," he replied, "that at the beginning the Creator 'made them male and female,' and said, 'For this reason a man will leave his father and mother and be united to his wife, and the two will become one flesh'? So they are no longer two, but one. Therefore what God has joined together, let man not separate." (Matthew 19:4–6).

After a couple of decades or so of trying to prove that men and women are essentially the same, scientific and mental health articles are now filled with the interesting "proof" that males and females are created very differently indeed. Secular pop psychology books set out to illustrate how men and women differ so much that you need to learn and understand the opposite sex's way of thinking before you can even begin to communicate. For example, what he sees as a power struggle, she feels is simply an expression of need.

If you deny each other your own uniqueness, it isn't a relationship but just two people living one life. . . . If our ideas and interests are rejected, we feel rejected.

He may think he doesn't need to say, "I love you, I'm sorry, I need you," because, after all, he's there, isn't he? At the same time, she will be absolutely sure that without the loving words, there are no loving feelings. When she says, "The children need you," she means for him to talk to them and give input in their lives. He thinks, "I just watched TV with them, didn't I?"

If male and female differences are not enough, when we marry, we blend an array of cultural and familial differences. Where to one partner yelling is perfectly normal, nonthreatening, and healthy, to another it is abuse simply because no one in her family ever did. One person may repress feelings and issues; another may be very confrontational. Your family may celebrate things in a big way while your spouse's family may try to always get by with as little fuss as possible. One of you likes country music, and one only listens to classical. Your spouse loves a certain holiday that you think is insignificant. You like to use blue in decorating, your spouse prefers green. You always have fresh veggies, your spouse never eats them.

Need I continue? Almost every aspect of daily living can be a potential disagreement. You can explore each other's worlds and open yourselves up to new ideas, new experiences, new techniques of living, or you can stubbornly cling to your own as the only way to live.

But God said, "Let the two become one," and we become one by totally entering into one another's worlds. If you never did "that," ate "that," heard "that" before, try it! Every time an issue of difference comes up between you, do your best to turn it into a time of growth and discovery instead of resistance and conflict.

You can continually make each other's tastes and habits seem inferior or dumb, or you can come to appreciate each other's tastes by trying everything. If you don't like it, at least you have experienced it once together.

In the October 1995 issue of *Focus on the Family Magazine*, Dr. Neil Warren writes, "Blending the uniqueness of one partner with the uniqueness of the other takes great skill, but the potential for a totally new corporate identity with maximum breadth and depth is an incredibly valuable goal to pursue."

He uses the example of music. Instead of handing out jabs and critical remarks about the other's music, say something like, "You know, Honey, you love country music and I love classical. I suspect that we could come to appreciate something in each other's taste if we worked at it a little. Would you listen with me if I listen with you?" He says that this strategy is designed to expand the boundaries of your life together and to increase the musical range of your relationship.

God brought together the two of you. You are unique and special people, different from each other and different from anyone else in the world. If you deny each other your own uniqueness, it isn't a relationship but just two people living one life. And within the person whose tastes and desires are ignored, there grows feelings of worthlessness and perhaps a sense of being unwanted. It is quite possible that the one who always has to "give up" his or her preferences will become convinced that he or she is in a loveless marriage. If our ideas and interests are rejected, we feel rejected.

In relating to our children, we point out to them how our differences make us better parents. "Dad is good at talking to you about thus and so, and I am good at doing this and that for you." We have taken our differences, our individual strengths, and made them a point of gratitude for our children, a way for them to appreciate both parents, whose differences assure the kids are being parented better than if we were the same. We also talk about their birthparent's qualities, how they were like or unlike us, and how that affected the kind of parent they were. What I hope they are learning is that all people, with their tastes, preferences, and personality traits, have value and can enrich our lives.

Let us strive to become truly one flesh with our mate, not by one person's giving up and giving in on everything, but by becoming a loving, caring duo interested in each other and concerned for one another's desires.

———◆———

Dear Creator God, thank You that You made us male and female and each one unique from the other. Help us to turn our differing tastes and individual approaches to life into occasions for discovery rather than rejection. May we learn to be two whole people who become one flesh, each one totally the person You intend, to make a whole marriage that will glorify You.
In Jesus' name, amen.

74
Fight the Good (?) Fight

◆

I have fought the good fight, I have finished the race, I have kept the faith
(2 Timothy 4:7).

So they are no longer two, but one. Therefore what God has joined together, let
man not separate (Matthew 19:6).

Do not let any unwholesome talk come out of your mouths, but only what is
helpful for building others up according to their needs, that it may benefit
those who listen (Ephesians 4:29).

Submit to one another out of reverence for Christ (Ephesians 5:21).

One way that we become separated in our marriages is through arguing and fighting. Face it, no two people, no matter how well intentioned or well matched, are going to agree on everything. The time comes when one of us will hurt or displease the other. Decisions will have to be made, and both of us will not necessarily agree.

> *The area of conflict resolution is the main reason, besides the children, that parents of a blended family may need to see a counselor.*

How a couple deals with conflict becomes an issue that can make or break the relationship. If you are divorced, lack of skill in conflict resolution may very well be the primary reason you ended your first marriage. Unfortunately, couples seem to follow patterns in their behavior. You may have trigger points that put you on the defensive and cause you to be combative. Thinking you are defending yourself, you lash out, and your spouse fights back when all along the spouse didn't think the issue offensive at all.

Failing to discover what your trigger points are and failing to break the downward cycle of negative conflict patterns can lead to mounting hostility and anger in the relationship. Hurt leads to more anger, and soon there may be an underlying resentment or bitterness that just never goes away.

One obvious way to minimize pain, which in turn minimizes anger, is to avoid things that hurt. No relationship should allow things like put-downs, name calling, or physical violence. To some couples shouting may be acceptable. But make sure that in shouting you are not hurting your spouse. You have to both agree that shouting is OK if it's not going to be hurtful.

Decide together what the rules of a fair fight may be. I use the word "fight" rather loosely when describing a marital conflict. You may say, "We never fight." Well, perhaps you don't yell or scream or throw things. But if you have ever had an emotional disagreement, we will call that a "fight."

The first rule of good fighting is to pick your issues carefully. Before you get confrontational, ask yourself, "Is this important enough to remember in a week? Six weeks? Six months? Is this an ongoing issue?"

Psychologist Dr. James Dobson shares some advice on this, "Try not to care so much about every minute detail that separates you and your loved ones. . . . Have you ever tried to recall a major fight you had . . . six months ago? It's very difficult to remember the details even a week later. The fiery intensity of one moment is a hazy memory of another."* So, don't make an issue of something that isn't important enough to be remembered.

In our marriage, in addition to the universal rules of fair fighting such as no name calling, no put-downs (otherwise known as character assassination), and no physical violence, we have acknowledged some things of our own to avoid. While the areas of pain to be avoided in a fight in your marriage may not be the exactly the same as ours, they very likely may be.

We try to not mention the previous spouse or the previous marriage in a fight, not dredge up the past in our own relationship (try to forget all that you have forgiven), and not make comparisons to our parents. I've heard comedy routines about the unforgivability of saying to a woman, "You're acting like your mother" or "Watch out! You're going to do what your mother did!"

I remember once snapping, "You're parenting just like your father!" It was amazing how fast "no parents in the fight" became our policy! Amazingly, these accusations don't have to be about anything specific or even have a particular parental behavior in mind. For whatever reason, they are just a jab that guarantees pain, and we have agreed not to do it.

Hurtful things that damage our loved one's sense of worth and especially make them feel unvalued by us may not be easy to spot. I doubt if you can sit down early in your marriage and say, "This and this and this really hurt me, so don't do them." As time goes on, though, you will see, if you're watching, what things come up often and how they cause pain. Call time out. Ask, "What does that have to do with the argument?" If they are items that always cause hurt and are not directly related to the conflict at hand, avoid them. The item you disagree on itself is probably difficult and painful enough without throwing out intentional barbs just to gain the upper hand.

Try to remember that you both want the winner to be *the relationship*, not one side or another. If you don't want a relationship marked by bitterness and unforgiveness, then look for those hurtful things that you need to avoid. If you don't learn to avoid them, one or both of you will often be on the defensive.

If you are always defending yourself, if you don't feel safe in your relationship, you will not be able to love. In order to have real intimacy, to be opened emotionally and physically, you need to feel safe, secure, and accepted.

The area of conflict resolution is the main reason, besides the children, that parents of a blended family may need to see a counselor. Many couples cannot find the pattern to their negative behavior, and some may not be able to understand, without help, how they are hurting their spouse.

We talked to one man that had never even considered the fact that the reason his wife was so angry was because she was hurting! When we pointed this out to him, he was amazed and also sorry. If he had interpreted her behavior as resulting from pain, he would have willingly made changes much sooner. If you can't find the source of your anger, if you don't see the patterns that always lead to conflict, get help. Don't allow anger and bitterness to eat away at your intimacy.

◆

*Dear Lord, please make us loving and sensitive spouses. May we never hurt one another on purpose. And when we do cause pain, help us to be quick to ask forgiveness. When we are hurt, help us to be honest about it and forgive. Thank You for Your healing power and Your awesome love at work in us.
In Jesus' name, amen.*

---

*Dr. James Dobson, *Love for a Lifetime* (Portland, Ore.: Multnomah Press, 1987), 116–17.

75

A Word from an Unmarried Ex-Spouse

◆

You are kind and forgiving, O Lord, abounding in love to all who call to you.
Hear my prayer, O LORD; listen to my cry for mercy. In the day of my trouble
I will call to you, for you will answer me (Psalm 86:5–7).

Be kind and compassionate to one another, forgiving each other, just as in
Christ God forgave you (Ephesians 4:32).

One Sunday morning in church as I greeted Brian, a single parent, it occurred to me that perhaps this unmarried ex-spouse, a man that shared his child with a blended family, may have a few things to say to stepparents. So I asked him to think about it. Being a thoughtful and caring person, he came up with some interesting comments.

> But the most pressing and urgent message to any stepparent remains: If you have not yet forgiven—do it! Only then can you really get on with your life.

The first thing Brian told me he needed when his marriage ended was what he suspects that all those who divorce need—forgiveness on both sides. He needed deeply and urgently to know that he was forgiven for anything he contributed to his wife's wanting to leave. He also needed her to know, just as deeply, that he forgave her for giving up on their marriage, something he never thought would happen. This was all years ago for Brian, and he is happy to say that long ago he and his wife reached this place of mutual forgiveness. But the most pressing and urgent message he would give to any stepparent remains: If you have not yet forgiven—do it! Only then can you really get on with your life.

He would like his ex-spouse to know that the hardest thing he ever did in all his life was to leave his child. His wife wanted to end the marriage so he had to go. But he also had to separate from the child who is his flesh and part of his heart. Did is ex-wife ever, he wonders, know how badly that hurt, how tough it was to leave their daughter? He truly had to learn to totally release his child to God, trusting in the Heavenly Father to be her parent when he wasn't there.

When his ex-wife remarried, he had to once again give up his child. Now another man would share in her daily life while he would only get every other weekend and some holidays. Not only did this involve letting her go again, but Brian had to trust another man, someone he didn't even know, to raise his daughter. It was scary as he once again gave his child to God. This time he had to trust not only in God and in his ex-wife, but he also had to learn to trust that new spouse.

Now that forgiveness is given and time has healed (which he says it does), he would like his ex-wife and her husband to know that even though he is still single, he does have a life and it is separate from theirs. He loves his child dearly and wants to be with her as much as possible, but he needs to be able to count on when she'll be with him, so he can make plans. He is there for his daughter with all his heart, but he has other obligations too, so please, consider this when you call upon him at an unspecified time.

"And please," he says, "have her ready to go when I come. The wounds have healed as much as they will. We are all nice and civil to one another. We have worked together successfully for many years now to mutually raise our child though we are not together. But do I really need to sit and wait for a half an hour in the living room of the home that could still be mine if you hadn't chosen otherwise? Think about those feelings when you know I'm coming, and please have her ready when I get there. Thank you."

For all of you stepparents to whom it applies, I hope that this word from a still-single ex-spouse will be helpful for you in gaining perspective on what things are like for him or her. Have you forgiven and been forgiven? Are there ways you could be more kind and thoughtful? If you wonder if any part of this man's story may apply to your ex-spouse—ask!

◆

Dear God, please help us to be able to forgive as You have forgiven us. Enable us to live in kindness and understanding with the parents of our children. May we be able to mirror Your love to them. In Jesus' name, amen.

76

What Is Good for the Goose May Not Be Good for the Gander

◆

Submit to one another out of reverence for Christ. Wives, submit to your husbands as to the Lord (Ephesians 5:21–22).

Husbands, love your wives, just as Christ loved the church and gave himself up for her (Ephesians 5:25).

Do nothing out of selfish ambition or vain conceit, but in humility consider others better than yourselves. Each of you should look not only to your own interests, but also to the interests of others. Your attitude should be the same as that of Christ Jesus (Philippians 2:3–5).

A popular radio counselor one day suggested a way to really love your wife as well as be a good father to your preschool children was to give your wife total time off—a night and day in a motel. She could work-out in the exercise room, take a long leisurely bath, read a book, and sleep all through the night without interruption. It sure sounds good to me! Take time off from responsibility? Just take care of myself for a whole twenty-four hours? Awe-

As we consider a way to meet our needs for rest and restoration, we need to think also of the rest and restoration of our relationship. Each of us needs to put the other first, scars, weaknesses, and all.

some! It's an especially good idea, I thought, if the children are preschoolers and the husband goes on hunting or fishing trips a lot or travels for his job.

Another lecturer believes that one person cannot possibly meet all the needs of another; women and men both need groups where they go for emotional and spiritual refreshment. In our culture women go to Bible studies, sororities, or Tupperware parties while men go to Bible studies, watch sporting events with a group, or spend the day hunting or fishing with a pal. This all sounds just fine to me too.

But as I related these ideas to my husband, he gently reminded me that all of these things would not be healthy and good for every marriage situation. We must consider our marriages first, he reminded me, and the emotional weaknesses of the person to whom we are married before we decide the best way to refresh and restore ourselves.

For example, in a relationship where trust is an issue, a husband might feel threatened if his wife went to a motel. Think about why his first marriage ended. Think, said my husband, about our friends whose marriage is recovering from an affair. The pain and subsequent scars may mean that sending a wife to a motel is not good for the relationship. What of the woman who was divorced because her husband spent all his time hunting and fishing and doing things with the boys until they had no shared life as a couple and no family life at all? She would probably feel really threatened when her new husband went off to do the same.

There are, after all, other ways to have time alone without going anywhere at all. Send the kids to a sitter or grandma or auntie. When Dad is home, go for a walk, visit the library, or soak in the tub, letting him attend to the kids. And what would be wrong with trading weekend child-care with another couple and getting away to the motel together rather than alone?

I agree with my husband that we need to be very careful about what we do for ourselves in a relationship. The above suggestions are great ideas for the right people. But as we consider a way to meet our need for rest and restoration, we need to think also of the rest and restoration of our relationship. Each of us needs to put the other first, scars, weaknesses, and all.

As we discover our spouse's old pains and spot insecurities that we didn't know existed before marriage, we can be reassuring, loving, and accepting. As we love, accept, and build our spouses up, we will see them become more secure in themselves and reassured in our marriages. Be cautious about accepting advice from experts on the radio or even from this book! Consider all in the light of what is good for your spouse—your marriage—you, the unique individuals that God has created you to be.

———————◆———————

Dear Jesus, please give us wisdom about how to do what is good for us and our souls and best for our marriages too. Thank You that You love us so much that You died for us, and may we be willing, each one of us, to give our lives for the other. In Jesus' name, amen.

77

Fear for Our Love—Tending Our Love

There is no fear in love. But perfect love drives out fear. We love because he first loved us (1 John 4:18a–19).

Love is patient, love is kind . . . Love does not delight in evil but rejoices with the truth. It always protects, always trusts, always hopes, always perseveres (1 Corinthians 13:4a, 6–7).

I feel afraid," I told my husband as I hugged him tightly.

"Of what?"

"I am afraid of all the badness," was my simplistic answer.

I had been talking to too many people about too many problems, both old and new. The weight of their burdens, their fear of the unknown in their marriages, their anger suppressed that I could feel, all these emotions took their toll, finally, on me.

I felt with them and hurt for them and entered into their emotions with them to the point that I had scared myself. I could see so easily how this or that happened! Yes, I could

If it always pains him for me to mention a certain thing, and if that thing has been dealt with as much as possible, then out of kindness, I should not mention it anymore. We hurt each other so many times in the past before we understood that some things just don't need to be said.

identify with him or her in that situation. I had begun to be afraid for our love and our marriage and our home simply by seeing up close all the things that could go wrong.

How fragile our love is. In some ways it is as delicate as a hothouse plant that requires careful tending. The wondrous thing is if we do tend it, if we do nurture it carefully, when the storms come, it will stand strong. What is this "tending" that makes love strong?

In our marriage, the love we share would not survive without being nurtured by our shared faith. Our faith is the greenhouse in which we planted the seed of our devotion to one another, the atmosphere in which we grow not only our relationship but our children. We both claim Jesus Christ as Lord. This means that we can pray together about our burdens. Our standards for our children, though they may vary some depending upon our families of origin, is at heart the same because we hold to the same guidebook for living—the Bible.

Because we claim the same Lord, we can pray together about our kids and any and all of our burdens. Praying together brings a special kind of intimacy like no other that I know. Ultimately, our love itself grows out of our love for God. Because as it says in 1 John 4:19 above, all love comes from God.

Another way that we tend to our love is by commitment. This doesn't just mean fidelity and the usual, "leaving all others . . ." It means no matter how tough a time we face, we are in this together. We are here for the long haul. And we have faced some really tough times. But when we remember that our first commitment (after God) is our commitment to our marriage, conflicts seem to gain perspective.

It helps a lot to remember that the most important element to the survival of our home and family is our couple love. There is no family, no home, without it. Sometimes we have been greatly divided because of the children, not agreeing on how to deal with certain issues. But rather than letting that drive us apart, we have learned to preserve our love and relent to the birthparent. Like anyone else, we've disagreed about any number of issues. But if we remember that we want our relationship to be the winner, not the issue or one of us, then we have a different view of the disagreement.

Commitment goes a long way in the nurturance and preservation of our love. If you are totally committed, if you know you aren't going anywhere, you will work a lot harder to keep where you are wonderful!

One of the ways that we "make it wonderful" is by simply being kind. Kind actions and kind words warm our love and make it grow the way the sun warms a flower and gently brings it to bloom. Open the door, help with the job, be patient for something to get done. Say "Please," say "I appreciate you," say "I love you." Say "You are so good for me because . . .," "You are great for the kids because . . .," "I'm sorry," and "I forgive you."

If it always pains him for me to mention a certain thing, and if that thing has been dealt with as much as possible, then out of kindness, I should not mention it anymore. We hurt each other so many times in the past before we understood that some things just don't need to be said. (I mentioned several of these in the rules for fair fighting, devotion 74.) I am NOT talking about unresolved issues. I am talking about things that have long ago been dealt with, decisions with the children long over with, old things, cold things, things that just don't need to be poured into the soil of our love anymore. They are dead and can become great fertilizer, but only if we let them rot away. I guess that a large part of kindness has to do with the way we communicate. To communicate our opinions and feelings clearly, without malice, can be like a good clean shower on the plant of our love. But all communication must be done in kindness.

I am absolutely sure that if we nurture our love with faith, commitment, and kindness, that delicate plant, so fragile that it will always need tending, will also be so strong that nothing can destroy it.

———◆———

Dear God, thank You for our love. Thank You so much for loving us first so that we can love each other. In Jesus' name, amen.

78
Acceptance: A Choice

◆

[The LORD] brought her to the man. The man said, "This is now bone of my bones and flesh of my flesh; she shall be called 'woman,' for she was taken out of man." For this reason a man will leave his father and mother and be united to his wife, and they will become one flesh. The man and his wife were both naked, and they felt no shame (Genesis 2:22b–25).

So they called Rebekah and asked her, "Will you go with this man?" "I will go," she said (Genesis 24:58).

Isaac brought her into the tent of his mother Sarah, and he married Rebekah. So she became his wife, and he loved her (Genesis 24:67a).

Adam accepted Eve not just because he liked the way she looked, but because God brought her to him. Isaac accepted a veiled Rebecca, brought to him by his father's servant who told him the story of how God led him to this woman. Our marriages are not arranged by our parents or our servants; God probably didn't come to you in person and "zap"

If we had known all the ways our spouse would eventually begin to "bug" us, if we had known all of his or her faults, we may have never married.

you with a revelation of who to marry. Instead we make a "love match," someone we accept and love in part because we picked them out ourselves.

Now we are married, and the time comes when our faults and bad habits begin to unveil themselves. No matter how honest we have been in dating, when we marry we will find weaknesses in our spouse. Perhaps their weaknesses will bring out the very worst in us!

The person of our dreams will not be a dreamboat after all—and this is true in ALL marriages. How do I know? Because there is simply no such thing as a perfect person. Studies have shown that even people who live together before marriage are not the same after they marry, and in fact those who have lived together beforehand have a higher rate of divorce than those who don't!

If we choose to continue in love and commitment despite the less-than-perfect character we discover in one another, we will also have to let go of any dreams we may have had for a "perfect" marriage. Two imperfect people simply cannot have a perfect relationship.

One marriage has ended. This next one is an attempt to "get it right this time," to make it work, to show the world that we are not failures, that we really are nice people and we can have a permanent relationship. So here we are. When we let go of that romanticized dream of the perfect relationship, we can begin to build a relationship that is unique, designed by God for just us.

If we had known all the ways our spouse would eventually begin to "bug" us, if we had known all of his or her faults, we may have never married. In our courtship it was easy to focus on all the things that we shared in common. Now it seems possible to see only what separates. Living for the rest of our lives in a successful relationship depends upon being able to accept and love one another—staying committed to each other despite the faults that have gradually been discovered—and re-learning to focus on the positive.

Think about Isaac and Rebekah again. They had never seen each other before. They accepted one another on the basis of what they were told by the servant that brought them together. Yet the verse says, "she became his wife and he loved her." I believe that Isaac made a conscious choice to love the wife that had been provided for him. We as imperfect humans must choose, perhaps daily, how to love, cherish, and remain committed to our imperfect spouses, and they to an imperfect us.

The popular marriage enrichment seminar known as "Marriage Encounter" teaches, "Love is a decision you make." I couldn't agree more. If you don't know how to remain committed, if you have a hard time loving despite the faults, I would encourage you to attend an Encounter Weekend. During one of these intense weekends, you will find how to communicate love and how to live a shared life rather than a life separated by differences.*

You may also benefit, as we have, from counseling, learning to understand and trust one another with the help of a go-between. But it still boils down to our choice—we choose to remain committed; we choose to put aside bitterness and forgive; we choose to love and accept our mate.

◆

Dear Father, teach us to love one another as You love us. May we accept our spouse and they us despite our faults, and may we build a marriage of Your design. In Jesus' name, amen.

---

*Denominational and nondenominational expressions of Marriage Encounter are available. Call World-Wide Marriage Encounter, 1-800-995-LOVE

79
Random Thoughts of Joy

◆

He prays to God and finds favor with him, he sees God's face and shouts for joy (Job 33:26a).

. . . the fruit of the Spirit is love, joy, peace . . . (Galatians 5:22a).

Your statutes are my heritage forever; they are the joy of my heart (Psalm 119:111).

As the Father has loved me, so have I loved you. Now remain in my love. If you obey my commands, you will remain in my love, just as I have obeyed my Father's commands and remain in his love. I have told you this so that my joy may be in you and that your joy may be complete. My command is this: Love each other as I have loved you (John 15:9–11).

I t was one of those great nights. Everyone seemed to be in a good mood. We shared our days with each other, laughed at every joke, and got so silly that first one and then another would burst out with a laugh, even during prayers! (I believe God enjoyed it too!) One time, I laughed so hard I actually had tears running down my cheeks. It was great! But face it, folks, this kind of harmony and unrelenting pure joy in

We may have pleasant enough evenings, but times of pure joy? They are rare. . . .No guilt, no shame, no pain that is not entrusted to His care, this is the beginning of joy.

each other's company does not happen often. We may have pleasant enough evenings, but times of pure joy? They are rare.

We would all like more joy in our homes. But where does it come from? How does it get there?

In the verses above I think it is quite clear that knowing God, "seeing His face," brings joy. How do we come to "see God's face?" We come to see God, to know God, by filling our hearts and our minds with His Word. Inner joy and peace begin with knowing God and knowing that we are right with God. No guilt, no shame, no pain that is not entrusted to His care, this is the beginning of joy. (See devotions 40–46 on the "New Life" for more details.)

C.S. Lewis wrote the story of his conversion and titled the book

Surprised by Joy, a description of what it felt like to go from a life of atheism to belief in God.* When the Holy Spirit lives within us, says Paul in Galatians, then we will have the fruit thereof, and joy is one of those fruits.

The Psalm above talks about finding joy in obedience to God's Word. Can you imagine? Being obedient brings joy! Ask your kids when they are happier: when there is harmony in your home or when there is strife? Joy comes with harmony. Of course we parents aren't as perfectly wise as God. Sometimes we don't know exactly what our children need, and so they may be frustrated by our expectations. But we can be sure that in obeying God is fullness of joy because the Bible says so, and God only expects what is good for us and knows exactly what we need.

The last verse quoted above mentions that Jesus came to bring us joy and encourages us again that if we obey Him, we will have joy. What command does He want us to obey? "To love one another."

So this joy comes from deep within us; this joy that can reside in our homes stems from love. First—God loved us. He loved us so much that Jesus gave His life for us. The Spirit lives within those who have invited Him in. Out of Spirit indwelt, obedient hearts, we love one another. And if, Jesus says, we obey Him by loving one another, we will have joy!

◆

Dear Lord Jesus, live within us. Give us obedient, loving hearts, that we may know real joy. In Your precious name, amen.

*C. S. Lewis, *Surprised by Joy* (New York: Harcourt, Brace and Jovanovich, 1984).

80
Another Day of Joy

◆

Nehemiah said, "Go and enjoy choice food and sweet drinks, and send some to those who have nothing prepared. This day is sacred to our Lord. Do not grieve, for the joy of the LORD is your strength" (Nehemiah 8:10).

Thou wilt show me the path of life: in thy presence is fullness of joy; at thy right hand there are pleasures for evermore (Psalm 16:11 KJV).

I n the book of Nehemiah, the people of God rebuilt the temple and restored the priesthood. Several years after the restoration, they gathered for the feast of the trumpets and also to hear the Word of the Lord read. It had been years since most of them had heard it. Many of them had been captives in Babylon and had not had access to God's Word.

Now, as God's Word went out to His regathered people, they understood that they had broken the law often and greatly strayed from His

Whether we have overtly disobeyed God's law, or whether we have simply fallen short of His ideal of treating one another with love and kindness, for whatever reason, we may be bowed down with a load of guilt.

will. Much grieved, they wept and mourned in the sorrow of their guilt.

But the prophet put an end to their weeping with these words: "The joy of the LORD is your strength." He wanted them to rejoice rather than sorrow, for now they knew what to do—now they knew how to obey. And they could find strength for obedience, he said, strength for living renewed lives in the *joy* of the Lord.

Whether we have overtly disobeyed God's law, or whether we have simply fallen short of His ideal of treating one another with love and kindness, for whatever reason, we may be bowed down with a load of guilt. But the Psalmist says, "In thy presence is fullness of joy." When we agree with God about our sin, the moment we ask His forgiveness, forgiveness is given and we are restored to His presence. In His presence not only do we find joy and "pleasures for evermore," but we also see that He will show us "the path of life." God's Word is a guide to all those who follow Him.

Let us be exhorted by the prophet and not dwell on our sins, weeping and anguishing over what we have done. Let us instead embrace His forgiveness and go on to live and walk in the joy of His presence.

———————◆———————

Dear Father God, thank You for sending Your Son to die so that I may be forgiven for my sins. Thank You that I do not have to dwell for even a moment on my sins, once I have been to You for forgiveness. Thank You that we can dwell in Your presence and trust that You have laid out a good path for our lives. May we walk with You every day and be filled with the joy of Your presence. In Jesus' name, amen.

81
Blessed Are the Meek

◆

... But the fruit of the spirit is love, joy, peace, patience, kindness, goodness, faithfulness, gentleness and self-control (Galatians 5:22–23a).

Blessed are the meek, for they will inherit the earth (Matthew 5:5).

Your beauty should not come from outward adornment, such as braided hair and the wearing of gold jewelry and fine clothes. Instead, it should be that of your inner self, the unfading beauty of a gentle and quiet spirit, which is of great worth in God's sight. For this is the way the holy women of the past who put their hope in God used to make themselves beautiful (1 Peter 3:3–5a).

The meekest, most self-controlled and gentle person I know is my Broersma mother-in-law. She is almost totally without malice. Even when others think she has a right to be angry, she

I couldn't imagine how his soft and gentle mom raised seven boys.

simply does not see the point of indulging herself in such emotion. This little woman, all five-feet-three of her, with a voice so soft I sometimes can't hear her clearly on the phone, successfully raised seven sons!

But when I once remarked to one of my brothers-in-law that I couldn't imagine how his soft and gentle mom raised seven boys, he cracked, "Are you kidding? She can jump-start a 747 and shaves her legs with a chain saw!!" That is how gentle he thought his mom was! But she didn't throw fits, and she didn't scream, and she largely left the corporal punishment to her husband.

So what was my brother-in-law talking about? What toughness did he sense in her that made him obey as a child and crack these jokes about her as an adult? I believe it was her simple strength of character. She was sure about right and wrong and had a clear idea of what she expected of her children. Her very attitude demanded respect and obedience. As she expected to be obeyed, she usually was.

My husband says, "Well, she may have been soft spoken, but she certainly had a fair amount of power to change things and get stuff done!" Besides, all of the boys agree, she had the backing of their dad one hundred percent. And any time they got in trouble with her or gave her a hard time, they knew dad was right behind her. And hey, who would argue with that?

She gives a lot of credit to God. When asked how she ever got through such and such a stage, she will often reply, "Well . . . that one took a lot of prayer." Her comment about relying upon the Lord through prayer is a good explanation of what the Scriptures refer to when speaking of meekness. No one can partake of God's grace, receive His forgiveness, "inherit the land" (be sure of eternal life), unless they are "meek" before God. Psalm 37:11 pictures the meek as those who trust in the Lord and commit their way to Him. This text assures us that it is the meek, those who have been humbled before God, that know with great surety that He will come to deliver and save them.

Jesus called Himself meek, saying, "Come unto me, all ye that labour and are heavy laden, and I will give you rest. Take my yoke upon you, and learn of me; for I am meek and lowly in heart: and ye shall find rest unto your souls" (Matthew 11:28–29 KJV). We are exhorted to be like Jesus, a Man who with humility accepted the will of God.

I, who am not meek by nature, ask myself if I have been humbled before God. Am I very aware that all I am and all I will be depends entirely upon His grace? Knowing that my life is utterly in His hands and that my salvation is by grace alone awes me and makes me indeed meek in heart. Only by coming to Him for salvation and accepting His "yoke," His will for my life, will I find rest and peace.

◆

Dear Jesus, help me, like You, to be humble and meek in spirit. May I live each day with the awareness that it is Your grace that brings me forgiveness, peace, and rest. Amen.

82
Why This Trial, Lord?

◆

To keep me from becoming conceited because of these surpassingly great revelations, there was given me a thorn in my flesh, a messenger of Satan, to torment me. Three times I pleaded with the Lord to take it away from me. But he said to me, "My grace is sufficient for you, for my power is made perfect in weakness." Therefore I will boast all the more gladly about my weaknesses, so that Christ's power may rest on me. That is why, for Christ's sake, I delight in weaknesses, in insults, in hardships, in persecutions, in difficulties. For when I am weak, then I am strong (2 Corinthians 12:7–10).

Stepparenting is a role that may well be plagued with seemingly endless and insurmountable difficulties and hardships.

If it is not a troubled or rejecting stepchild, it may be an ex-spouse who interferes too much or doesn't do his or her share of child-rearing at all—just enough to mess up what you're trying to accomplish. Maybe you or your child has a physical ailment that simply will not go away. How does one cope? How do you remain faithful even when you feel like throwing in the towel?

"I just don't want to do this anymore. I just can't take being this messed up kid's parent any longer! The pressure is too great."

If you're thinking, "I just don't want to do this anymore. I just can't take being this messed up kid's parent any longer! The pressure is too great," then be assured—many stepparents have those feelings. When you're at the end of all your strength, it is not wrong to have those feelings. But there is all the difference in the universe between feeling like that and doing it.

You may feel like giving up, but you can still choose to be committed and loving. The apostle Paul wrote of weaknesses, insults, and hardships that were so bad he wanted to give up. But instead, he said, his times of not feeling up to the job, his times of weakness, became the time that Christ's strength could take over in him. For when the apostle was weakest were the times when Christ had an opportunity to be the strength of his life.

I challenge you stepparents who may feel discouraged, who may feel utterly defeated, to come to Jesus with every bit of your brokenhearted despair. Give it to Him. Tell Him you have had enough, you can't do anymore, and that He will have to love the kids through you because you just don't have it right now. I know from experience that from that pitiable state, He truly can come and give you a shot of His love and kindness. And His grace truly is sufficient! Please—tap into His supply of grace. You will find that His grace is sufficient for you.

◆

Dear Lord God, may all who read this book truly experience the apostle's discovery, that Your power can be made perfect in our weakness. May we simply let go, and let You be God in us. Amen.

83

Testing Brings Forth Faith—Pure As Gold

◆

But he knows the way I take; when he has tested me, I will come forth as gold (Job 23:10).

In this you greatly rejoice, though now for a little while you may have had to suffer grief in all kinds of trials. These have come so that your faith—of greater worth than gold, which perishes even though refined by fire—may be proved genuine and may result in praise, glory and honor when Jesus Christ is revealed (1 Peter 1:6–7).

For our light and momentary troubles are achieving for us an eternal glory that far outweighs them all. So we fix our eyes not on what is seen, but on what is unseen. For what is seen is temporary, but what is unseen is eternal (2 Corinthians 4:17–18).

Learning to find strength when we are weak is not the only good thing that can happen to stepparents under stress. When we are stressed and we remain faithful, when others see that Christ is at work in us doing what we could not be doing on our own, we are puri-

Faith that has not been tested is no faith at all, for what is faith but confidence in what we have not seen?

fying our faith—demonstrating to ourselves, our family, and the world around us that our faith is real, that He is at work.

When the stress eases, you will say, "He has held me up and kept me going when I had no more patience and no more love. I trusted in Him, and He is real, folks. He really does give strength for the day when I have none, patience for the situation that seems hopeless." And even before an end is in sight, others know that your faith is real because you don't give up, you don't leave. And you don't hate; you do love. His strength made perfect in your weakness proves that this God in Whom you have put your trust is real, alive, and involved day-to-day in this stepparenting life.

Faith that has not been tested is no faith at all, for what is faith but confidence in what we have not seen? Faith happens when life seems the most grim, when we see no answers to our dilemmas, when we're sure that we can't go on, when there's no reason to think positively. But we do go on, and we can survive, and we do find joy, and that is how we deal with "it" even without answers because as we live, we have learned that He is real. He is there; He supplies every need for love, for comfort, for strength.

And the most glorious thing of all is that all of these trials, every pain, every frustration of parenting, stepparenting, second marriages, all the tough stuff of blending a family, no matter how bad it is or how difficult it gets, none of it weighs as much as the awesome glory and the all-surpassing, all-encompassing joy that we will know in an eternity with our precious Savior, Jesus Christ.

◆

Dear Lord, make our faith strong. May we be tested in the fire and come out refined as the purest gold. May we show through all of our lives that our faith is real. In the awesome and powerful and eternal name of Jesus we pray, amen.

84
The All-Sufficient God

◆

*When Abram was ninety-nine years old, the LORD appeared to him and said,
"I am God Almighty; walk before me and be blameless. I will confirm my
covenant between me and you and will greatly increase your numbers." Abram
fell facedown (Genesis 17:1–3a).*

*Whom have I in heaven but you? And being with you, I desire nothing on
earth. My flesh and my heart may fail, but God is the strength of my heart
and my portion forever (Psalm 73:25–26).*

I have mentioned many times in this book the importance of maintaining a quality marriage relationship. From the love and nurturing of one's spouse, a stepmom or stepdad can be built up in the love and patience needed to be a good

*Are the children more
than you can handle?
Do you feel over-
whelmed and alone?*

parent. But realistically, no one is perfect, and no one person, not even a loving spouse, can possibly meet every emotional and spiritual need.

At a very needy time in Abram's life, when he was despairing of ever seeing God's promises fulfilled for him, God appeared to Abram and announced, "I am God Almighty!" This name for God, literally, "El Shaddai," means more than just God of power and might. It means that God is the All-Sufficient One, the provider of all that we are and all that we need.

Abram appropriately fell flat on his face before El Shaddai, and from his position of conscious humility and profound reverence, he worshiped the All-Sufficient God, the One who held his very life in His hands. This God had come to restore life to Abram's dried-out, old body and make fertile the womb of his elderly wife, Sarai. In keeping with this renewal, He gave them new names, "Abraham" and "Sarah," the parents of many nations. God would give them a son from whom would come a great nation, a people through whom would come the salvation of the world.

What a way for God to demonstrate His all-sufficiency! If He can put life in a barren womb, if He can grow the great nation of Israel out of one man's single offspring, then there is nothing that He cannot provide, including strength for my day, patience for my trying times, and love when there is none naturally. God can truly be my All-Sufficient

One when I humble myself before Him and willingly receive His portion, His will for me.

When the Psalmist wrote that God was his strength and his portion forever, he meant that God was all that he had and all that he needed. Oh that I would be more aware of God's power and strength in my life! How often I try to live and work on my own and in my own strength. But the All-Sufficient God is always there, offering His strength in my weakness (2 Corinthians 12:9).

Are the children more than you can handle? Does your spouse seem remote and uncommunicative when you really need him or her to hold you or listen to you? Do you feel overwhelmed and alone? God is the All-Sufficient One. Like Abram, fall flat on your face before Him. In humility and reverence praise Him for all that He is and all that He has done. Call upon Him for strength, as the Psalmist did. He will answer and show you great and wondrous things that you cannot even imagine (Jeremiah 33:3).

◆

Dear God, All-Sufficient One, thank You for life and breath. Please fill me with Your love and give me strength to be a stepparent. Thank You. In the name of Your Son, Jesus Christ, who overcame death and brings life to me, I pray, amen.

85
The Power of a Kind Word

◆

An anxious heart weighs a man down, but a kind word cheers him up (Proverbs 12:25).

The tongue has the power of life and death, and those who love it will eat its fruit (Proverbs 18:21).

Do not let any unwholesome talk come out of your mouths, but only what is helpful for building others up according to their needs, that it may benefit those who listen (Ephesians 4:29).

You know the kind of day. Your husband comes home silent, head down. He sits at the table quietly, doesn't joke around, and acts removed. A touch, a kind word. "Tough day?" And soon he's explaining a little about the worries and pressures of the job. After a few

Sometimes you are amazed at how a few kind words can light up his face and draw him out.

moments of relaxation during which you may tell him that you appreciate him for thus and so, or that you admire him, he begins to seem more relaxed. Sometimes you are amazed at how a few kind words can light up his face and draw him out.

Perhaps you are the one weighted down. Perhaps you are frustrated that nothing at all has gone well today. Maybe you feel like a failure, or maybe you just feel like the world of kids and grannies and your own job is stockpiling against you. And unexpectedly your husband tells you the dinner is good or that you look nice. Suddenly, there is a glimmer of sunshine behind the clouds and you feel your mood shift, if not to complete cheerfulness, at least to a more positive outlook.

What brought these changes, these glimmers of hope and almost joy in an otherwise gloomy time? A kind word! How often both husband and wife are oblivious to the moods and needs of their spouses. We tend to say, "Hi, honey, you'll never believe what that kid did today" or "Guess what's broken now?!" He may come in and say, "Why are my tools out in the driveway? Whose bike was blocking my way?"

These and many other items of greater and lesser consequence are all things that of course need to be addressed and dealt with, unfortunately often at the end of the day. But time, place, and sensitivity should all come into play. Be sensitive to how your spouse feels when you meet at the end of the day. Be kind and patient, not dumping all at once, but gradually, throughout the evening, discuss the necessary.

Each irritation and problem is easier to deal with if couched in kind words, encouragement for the day's challenges, and positive comments about our spouse's accomplishments. "Be kind and compassionate to one another . . ." (Ephesians 4:32). These are great words to remember. Nothing is as powerful as words for making or breaking the esteem and spirit of our spouse. Will we choose words that weigh down or a kind word that lifts up? How will we speak today?

◆

Dear God, please help us use our words to encourage and lift up our spouse and our children. Help us to be kind. When we don't feel loving, help us to rely upon You to give us the love and patience that we need. May both the husband and wife of this home speak kindly and tenderly to the other. By doing this, may others see You at work in our relationship. In Jesus' name and for His glory we ask this, amen.

86
Guaranteed Love

♦

And you also were included in Christ when you heard the word of truth, the gospel of your salvation. Having believed, you were marked in him with a seal, the promised Holy Spirit, who is a deposit guaranteeing our inheritance until the redemption of those who are God's possession—to the praise of his glory (Ephesians 1:13–14).

Love is made complete among us so that we will have confidence on the day of judgment, because in the world we are like him. There is no fear in love. But perfect love drives out fear (1 John 4:17–18a).

Neither party in a marriage is perfect. We will not always speak kindly to one another. We will not always handle differences and irritations with gentleness. Sometimes we may think that our spouse is the biggest meany or the most selfish person that we ever knew! But you know what? If we are children of God, then we are still children of God even when we sin.

> *How much would our commitment and love be worth if it were only valid when our spouse was acting perfectly?*

We need to deal with one another in the loving and forgiving way that God deals with us. There will be a judgment, but Christ has already paid for our sins through His blood to settle that judgment. He paid because of His great love for us, and "perfect love drives out fear." Although we may grieve Him, or even make Him angry, we don't have to be afraid that God will ever stop loving us.

The Ephesians passage above tells us that our being included in Christ was assured when we heard and believed the truth about salvation. We are sealed; the ownership of our souls by God is guaranteed by the "seal" or the mark of the Holy Spirit. Even if we do fall short of being the kind of husband or wife that we know God wants us to be, we can be forgiven, and we are still guaranteed our inheritance in Christ.

The verse from 1 John reminds us that we are God's representatives of love in this world and that perfect love casts out all fear. Both of these verses speak of the need to assure our mates of our commitment, loyalty, and love regardless of their performance on a certain day. How much would our commitment and love be worth if it were only valid when our spouse was acting perfectly?

We can certainly be honest and tell our spouse that we feel hurt or disappointed about something he or she may have said or done. But we also need to communicate the fact that his or her worth and value as a person does not depend on always perfect behavior. Our worth and value depend on the fact that we are created in the image of God and that we are persons for whom Christ died. Because we may fail, it does not mean we are total failures or worthless people.

We want our spouse to be forgiving and understanding when we are less than we should be; we need to treat our spouse with the kind of love that casts out all fear of rejection or judgment. If God is willing to guarantee our salvation in Christ to the point that He will seal us, put a mark on us proving ownership despite the fact that we still have a whole life to live and many mistakes to make, we should likewise be willing to guarantee to our spouse that we will love, accept, and forgive, even when he or she is not perfect.

◆

Dear merciful, gracious, kind and loving God, thank You that You always expect the best from us. Thank You that You also forgive us when we are not our best. May we not be sloppy or lazy about obedience, thinking, "Oh well, we are forgiven." Help us to be serious about obeying You. But when we do sin and as our spouse sins against us, help us to be forgiving. Help us to relate to one another consistently, not for what we do but for who we are in Christ Jesus. Then may others know we are Christians by our love for You and our love for each other In Jesus' name, amen.

87
Food for the Soul

◆

[Jesus said,] "Do not work for the food that perishes, but for the food that endures for eternal life" (John 6:27a NRSV).

[The LORD] humbled you by letting you hunger, then by feeding you with manna, with which neither you nor your ancestors were acquainted, in order to make you understand that one does not live by bread alone, but by every word that comes from the mouth of the LORD (Deuteronomy 8:3 NRSV).

Then Jesus declared, "I am the bread of life. He who comes to me will never go hungry, and he who believes in me will never be thirsty (John 6:35).

The man without the Spirit does not accept the things that come from the Spirit of God, for they are foolishness to him, and he cannot understand them, because they are spiritually discerned (1 Corinthians 2:14).

Parenting is awesome, challenging, and rewarding—stepparenting is many times more challenging. The challenges and trials of stepparenting are what make the awe so tremendous when we are surprised by the love that may finally grow up between stepparent and stepchild. While waiting for the "awe," when attempting to do the right thing and be the right kind

There is no such thing as having someone else partake of food and drink for my good. Standing and watching others eat will not supply my needs.

of parent, where is a stepparent to go for hope and strength? I have said it before and I will say it again—the way to stay full of encouragement, the way to renew strength, to gain wisdom, to grow in love is to eat continually of the Word of God. The food of the Scripture provides not only the strength and wisdom to be a stepparent but also the source of all the soul craves. "He that comes to me," says Christ, "will hunger and thirst no more." When we feast on Jesus, the longings of our souls are satisfied.

Because this book is about hope and encouragement for the challenges of stepparenting, I can't help but emphasize the source of all hope: Jesus, the Bread of Life. Arthur Pink, in his *Exposition of the Gospel of John*, reminds us that eating is an intensely personal act; it is something which no one else can do for us. There is no such thing as having someone else partake of food and drink for my good. Standing and watching others eat will not supply *my* needs. No one can believe in Christ for me or gain strength from the Scripture on my behalf. I must take time to consider what I read in God's Word. I must apply it to my life. The deep hunger of my soul eases as I enjoy fellowship and communion with the Living God.*

Unless you have "eaten" the Bread of Life, unless you have personally said to Jesus, "Yes, I make You my Lord," you will not have sins forgiven, life in heaven, and the Holy Spirit within. It is having the Spirit that enables one to receive encouragement and strength from the Word. I pray that all who read this book will have partaken of Jesus, the Bread of Life, and having filled themselves with Him, go on to daily feast of the bread of His Word.

———————◆———————

Dear Lord Jesus, may we eat and drink daily of Your Word. May we know what it is to have the soul's hunger and thirst satisfied by the truth of Your Word, the Bible. Thank You for the Spirit that reveals all truth.
In Jesus' name, amen.

———————

*Arthur Pink, *Exposition of the Gospel of John* (Grand Rapids: Zondervan, 1974), 326.

88
The Blended Empty Nest

♦

"For I know the plans I have for you," declares the LORD, "plans to prosper you and not to harm you, plans to give you hope and a future"
(Jeremiah 29:11).

Her children arise and call her blessed; her husband also, and he praises her: "Many women do noble things, but you surpass them all." Charm is deceptive, and beauty is fleeting; but a woman who fears the LORD is to be praised. Give her the reward she has earned, and let her works bring her praise at the city gate (Proverbs 31:28–31).

I n all my conversations with step-parents, I have discovered many different kinds of blended families. Most are blended from divorce. A few, like us, were blended from death. Every blended family has challenges and trials unique to their own special "blend." Do you ever wonder how this will all turn out?

Recently I talked to Deborah, a woman who is at the reward stage of her blended-family experience— a mom with kids all grown—a grandmother to many. She looks back on her life as a mom and step-mom realistically. Deborah does not deny the struggles but is also quick to point out the great stuff— the rewards that came along.

The hardest thing of all, most stepparents agree, is the disciplining of each other's children. . . . Make sure that in all the struggles with the kids you take time for your couple relationship. That is what the home is built on and that is what you will have when the kids are gone.

She says the best part is now—finally alone with the man she loves, able to enjoy their grown children, birth and stepchildren alike. Looking back, she says initially the best thing about being a stepparent was being there for all those needy, hurting children.

Deborah was widowed and a single mom to a son and two daughters. She married Phil within a year of his first wife's death and felt privileged to step in and be a mom to his two daughters and son. She says she saw that they were hurting so much. She felt compassion for them and a desire to be the one to love away their pain. And she was able to. But, she says, the love did not come automatically. She had to win their trust, and time had to pass before love between them could blossom and grow.

Suddenly doubling her family meant there were many moments when Deborah felt like a slave: washing, ironing, and cooking without end and still hearing some complaints. Kids the ages of theirs did not necessarily appreciate all that she did. During those times of being bowed under with all the work, it was her husband's love that kept her going. They always took time to date each other. They took dance lessons together and tried to go out to dinner and talk at least once a week. As much as she loves all the children, Deborah says these times of coupleness were the thing that made it all possible, the thing that kept them going in the face of all the challenges presented by the blended family.

The hardest thing of all, she feels, and most stepparents agree, is the disciplining of each other's children. Without an emotional history, the stepparent just doesn't understand the kids like a birthparent does, which makes it hard to know the right thing to do. Sometimes, Deborah recalls, she would find herself silent, although she had previously not thought she was the silent type, simply because she didn't know what to say or how to deal with the child presenting the problem. But she also realized the lack of emotional attachment helped her be a more objective disciplinarian. You tend, she said, to be more tolerant of misdeeds in your own children, and the others are quick to point out any inequities! She said they had to pray a lot about their discipline situations. Then she recalled for me how those prayers were answered.

She often had trouble with her eleven-year-old stepson, Donald, the one child who would say, "You're not my mom so I don't have to do what you say." Finally the day came when Phil was home when Donald went into a yelling tirade of disobedience against his stepmother. Deborah recalls with appreciation how her husband backed her one hundred percent and made Donald understand in no uncertain terms that this woman was his wife and the mother of this house. Donald would do as he was told. From then on he did—as much as any kid would. Deborah says each of their children in their own way had to come to a place of accepting the stepparent.

Her teenage son, Jacob, had even a tougher adjustment. Jacob had an extremely hard time accepting his stepfather's interference in his life. Phil tried to back off and let Deborah handle this particular kid as much as possible, but there were times when he just had to be involved. They were several years into their marriage on the traumatic day that Jacob vented all his anger against Phil. It was an awful few minutes as these two men, one a son and one a stepfather, actually became physically violent. As they wrestled and punched, they told each other how hard they were to live with, but they came out of it understanding that they had to learn to do it anyway. They got out all their feelings. Deborah says that after this airing of all the pent-up rage, there was never a problem between them again. After this Jacob began to call his stepfather "pop"—an awesome title for this family as it showed that the stepfather had not taken the place of the birthfather in the child's heart, but he had won a place of special parenthood all his own.

Now, says this mom-stepmom-grandmother, the biggest joy, other than being alone with her husband, is the family reunions. All the grand-children love to come to this grandma's house, and her children and stepchildren as well rise up and call her blessed. They are thankful for her years of stepping into the gap, filling in the void, giving herself to them, and loving them into the whole adults that they have become.

I would hope that any who read this book will not give up on the toughest adjustments in your blended-family story. Seek help as needed, remain united and committed as you move your children on to adult-hood. And, as Deborah reflects, make sure that in all the struggles with the kids, you take time for your couple relationship. That is what the home is built on, and that is what you will have when the kids are gone.

◆

Dear Sovereign One, Ruler of the lives of Your children, we thank You for the plans You have for us, though they often are not what we expect. In it all You are faithful toward us, and we thank You. In Jesus' name, amen.

89
God—the Perfect Parent

◆

The LORD your God is with you, he is mighty to save. He will take great delight in you, he will quiet you with his love, he will rejoice over you with singing (Zephaniah 3:17).

The eternal God is your refuge, and underneath [you] are the everlasting arms (Deuteronomy 33:27a).

He tends his flock like a shepherd: He gathers the lambs in his arms and carries them close to his heart; he gently leads those that have young (Isaiah 40:11).

Some people have trouble trusting God with their lives, with their "real selves," because God is "God the Father." They have been abused or emotionally harmed by their physical fathers. But verses like the three above are magnificent depictions of a gentle, nurturing God—the perfect parent.

So often we need to stop wrestling with the circumstances of our lives and nestle in the arms of God.

Some people would say that these pictures of such a nurturing God are showing us "God as mother." They believe that we should then address God as "mother" sometimes so that we can know and understand that He is the gentle, caring, all-sufficient nurturing mother that we need. But this approach is a truly sexist attitude. Cannot a father, a perfect father, be the perfect nurturing parent? God has chosen in His Word to call Himself "our Father." And at the same time, He has given us pictures of what a perfect father is: one who gently holds us in his arms, who carries us when we need strength, who quiets us when our minds are in turmoil, who literally nestles us close to his heart.

I've seen mothers who hold their young babies at arm's length, who feed bottles while balancing their child on their knees, who cannot seem to cuddle or hold the little one near their heart. I've seen fathers who love the softness of their babies and hold them close indeed. I know a dad who kissed the top of his son's fuzzy head whenever it passed his chin, which was often, as he always held his baby close. So it isn't an issue of mother or father. It is an issue of God, the perfect parent, being exactly what we need. He is God our heavenly Father, and He has shown us in His Word exactly what a perfect father does: He cares for us, nurtures us, disciplines us, and never ever lets us out of his loving care.

My Smith mother-in-law recently reminded me that Corrie ten Boom, a prisoner in the concentration camps of World War II, was known to say, "Don't wrestle, just nestle." So often we need to stop wrestling with the circumstances of our lives and nestle in the arms of God. There is so much He can teach us, so much love He wants to give us, so much nurturing, guidance, and strength He wants to feed us. But if we are squirming and fighting to get out of His arms and on our own, if we rebel against His will and Word, we will never have peace. We stepparents will be better parents if we are parented well ourselves, and God wants to do that parenting. Will we let Him? God, the perfect parent, loves us and wants to hold us in His arms. All we need do is nestle there—and find perfect love and peace.

◆

Dear Heavenly Father, thank You that You are the perfect Parent, full of love, all-sufficient, never failing Father. Thank You for caring for me. Thank You for adopting me as Your child and for holding me in Your everlasting arms.
I love You. May I learn from You how to love my children.
In the name of Jesus, my Savior, my Friend, amen.

90
The Lord That Heals

◆

... for I am the LORD that healeth thee (Exodus 15:26b KJV).

... to comfort all who mourn, and provide for those who grieve in Zion—to
bestow on them a crown of beauty instead of ashes, the oil of gladness instead
of mourning, and a garment of praise instead of a spirit of despair. They will
be called oaks of righteousness, a planting of the LORD (Isaiah 61:2b–3).

Call unto me, and I will answer thee, and show thee great and mighty things,
which thou knowest not (Jeremiah 33:3 KJV).

I have written much in this book about the trials and adjustments of both parents and children when blending families. I have written several times about the wisdom of getting professional help and group support when needed for understanding, strength, and healing. I hope that I have emphasized even more the healing power and sustaining strength of the Lord God.

If you get nothing else from this devotional book, I hope that you will believe in the power of God to bring a resurrection, a new life, to you.

He can take a brokenhearted child and, loving that child through you, heal the wounds. He can take an adult from the clutches of an alcohol addiction that ruined a first marriage. That person becomes new, living in victory and successful in a new marriage. God can bring forgiveness and wholeness to anyone who asks.

I was reminded recently that it is the power of the Resurrection that makes one new in Christ. Baptism by immersion is a beautiful illustration of this: dead and buried to sin (immersed under the water), resurrected (raised out of the water) to a new life in Christ. This ceremony is a picture of the work of God in the individual, and the baptism is done "in the name of the Father, the Son, and the Holy Spirit."

God offers salvation through Jesus Christ, and the Holy Spirit makes people new and gives them power over the sin. That power includes not only forgiveness for misdeeds and wrong attitudes of the heart, but also comfort for grief, healing for pain, and release from addictions. To receive His forgiveness is to begin a healing that can go on to include all areas of one's existence. I love the line from the old hymn, "All my guilt and despair, Jesus took on Him there, for Calvary *covered it all.*"

Counselors are great for getting to the root of the problem in a hurting child; support groups such as Al-anon and Alcoholics Anonymous bring flesh and blood support to those who need it. But it is God's love and grace that heals; in His Word is wisdom. These all combine with the supernatural mighty power of the Spirit to make all things new. This is a power that is bigger than any betrayal, grace that is greater than any sin, strength that is mightier than the hold of any addiction, love and comfort that is deeper than any grief. If you get nothing else from this devotional book, I hope that you will believe in the power of God to bring a resurrection, a new life, to you.

◆

Thank You, dear God, for giving us Your love through Your Son. Thank You for the power of His resurrection, available to us. May we live as people who have died and been raised to a new life in Christ. In Jesus' name, amen.

Epilogue:
Letters from Margaret and Roger

◆

I can do all things through Christ, which strengtheneth me
(Phillipians 4:13 KJV).

To Moms and Stepmoms from Margaret:

If you read the biographical information on the back of this book, you may think that Margaret Smith-Broersma is some kind of "supermom." I want to assure you that I am not! I am an ordinary woman with some very real physical limitations. My secret to accomplishing a variety of things is simply doing them one at a time.

I was a stay-at-home mom during my childrens' early years. When the boys were little, I did the homey things I had always wanted to do, like needlepoint, sewing, and making bread. When I suddenly acquired three more children and more than doubled my extended family, I gave up the crafts and sewing and didn't know what it meant to have any "free time" at all for several years! Just being a mom, doing school and church activities, and giving all the grandmothers some time were all I could handle for awhile. I only began Bible teaching and public speaking gradually, as the children got older.

This single-mindedness served me well when I went to graduate school. At that time I dropped all my other outside projects, including speaking engagements and jobs at church. All I did was school (one class at a time) and kids. And even when I was asked to write my first book, I felt I had to put my publisher on "hold" while I finished a class. Now I only teach one class when writing a book and only teach more if I'm not writing. I speak only once in awhile—all of the time keeping in mind the needs of my now teenage children (with two out of high school).

Moms, I believe you and I live in a wonderful age for women. We can "have it all and do it all," but we don't have to do it all at once! We will probably live long enough to try everything we'd like if we have a plan, are patient for the right timing, and are very careful of priorities. And for those of you who have to do it all at once, who have to work full-time while parenting young children, I say, "Don't try to be perfect!" It is not possible to do it all and do it perfectly.

My prayer for all of you is that you will enjoy every stage of your life, doing what you know is right for you and your family before God.

Don't ever be intimidated or awed by someone else's life; instead, live your own to the fullest, using all the gifts and talents God has given you. Matthew 25:14–30 says the more you faithfully use the talents you have, the more you'll get—it's a promise!

◆

To Dads and Stepdads from Roger:

Many fathers go into a remarriage with an idealistic, "Brady Bunch" view of how the new family will be. They may think something like, "With this new wife, with our more perfect love, this marriage is going to be great!" But any family, particularly a blended one, is complex—intertwined with all kinds of emotional pains and needs. God's love and power, and possibly outside help, are needed to make a stepmom and dad and all the children into a healthy family unit. There are hurts, disappointments, and other deep feelings, some of which are so hidden they refuse to be named. As dads, we may want to ignore or hide from these things. But we can't. If we do ignore unresolved issues, it will be to the detriment of our families and marriages.

I was fortunate in that a friend of mine, Rev. Jerry Alferink, warned me that "blending" would be difficult. He told me that he had counseled many blended families and that they often didn't make it. This was tough to hear, but it helped me have a more realistic view going in. When things didn't work out "television perfect" at first, I wasn't taken by surprise. Knowing that struggles and conflicts are normal and that we could expect to need outside help to get through the rough spots motivated us to get that help when we needed it, before irreparable damage was done to our relationships.

Now many years later, we have, in my view, a very nice family unit. Many people we meet don't have any idea we are a blended family until they start to wonder why all our kids are almost the same age. And even when they get to know us well, they sometimes forget which kids are the biological children of whom.

Last week we celebrated our youngest son's seventeenth birthday, and the whole family was home, including the two college teens who came with an extra boyfriend and girlfriend. It gave me a warm feeling to see the whole family together and watch them interact. By just looking at them all, I could see how God has answered many of our prayers. For this we are eternally thankful. We are still praying that all of our children will grow up to be the men and women God wants them to be, and if they marry, to marry the person God has chosen for them. I can't wait to see how it will all turn out!

I would like to tell every dad who is also a stepdad, don't try to be "Super Dad." Don't worry about meeting some radio or TV person's image. Don't. You will never even come close to measuring up. You must, however, be humble and rely on God to give you strength, because no man can love his wife, children, and stepchildren perfectly. But God can. And if we call on Him, He can help us love more perfectly. If you try to love on your own, your family may be one of the many casualties of a remarriage with children. But love with God's love, and you have the best chance to make your new family truly a "blended one."

◆

Also by Margaret Smith-Broersma

Devotions for the Blended Family
Living and Loving as a New Family

T his unique book provides 152 devotions to affirm each other, discuss problems and successes, and to celebrate the unity of the new, blended family. Designed to be used by parents and children together, *Devotions for the Blended Family* includes a daily Bible reading and discussion of a relevant family topic. Also included are questions for further family interaction.

Margaret and her husband, Roger, have found that many of their most successful times of healing, adjustment, and growth as a family have come from their daily devotion time together around the table after the evening meal. This book gives an honest and hope-filled expression to the struggles and triumphs of a blended family.

ISBN 0-8254-2150-0

Available at your Christian bookstore or
by calling 1-800-733-2607